THE ILLUSTRATED STEPHEN KING TRIVIA BOOK

Edited by Brian Freeman and Bev Vincent

Illustrated by Glenn Chadbourne

With a special afterword by
Michelle L. Revelle
SKEMERs Founder/Co-President

CEMETERY DANCE PUBLICATIONS

Baltimore

❖ 2005 ❖

Trade Hardcover Edition ISBN 1-58767-116-6
Trade Paperback Edition ISBN 1-58767-108-5

THE ILLUSTRATED STEPHEN KING TRIVIA BOOK

Manufactured in the United States of America.

FIRST EDITION

Cemetery Dance Publications
132-B Industry Lane
Unit 7
Forest Hill, MD 21050
Email: info@cemeterydance.com

www.cemeterydance.com

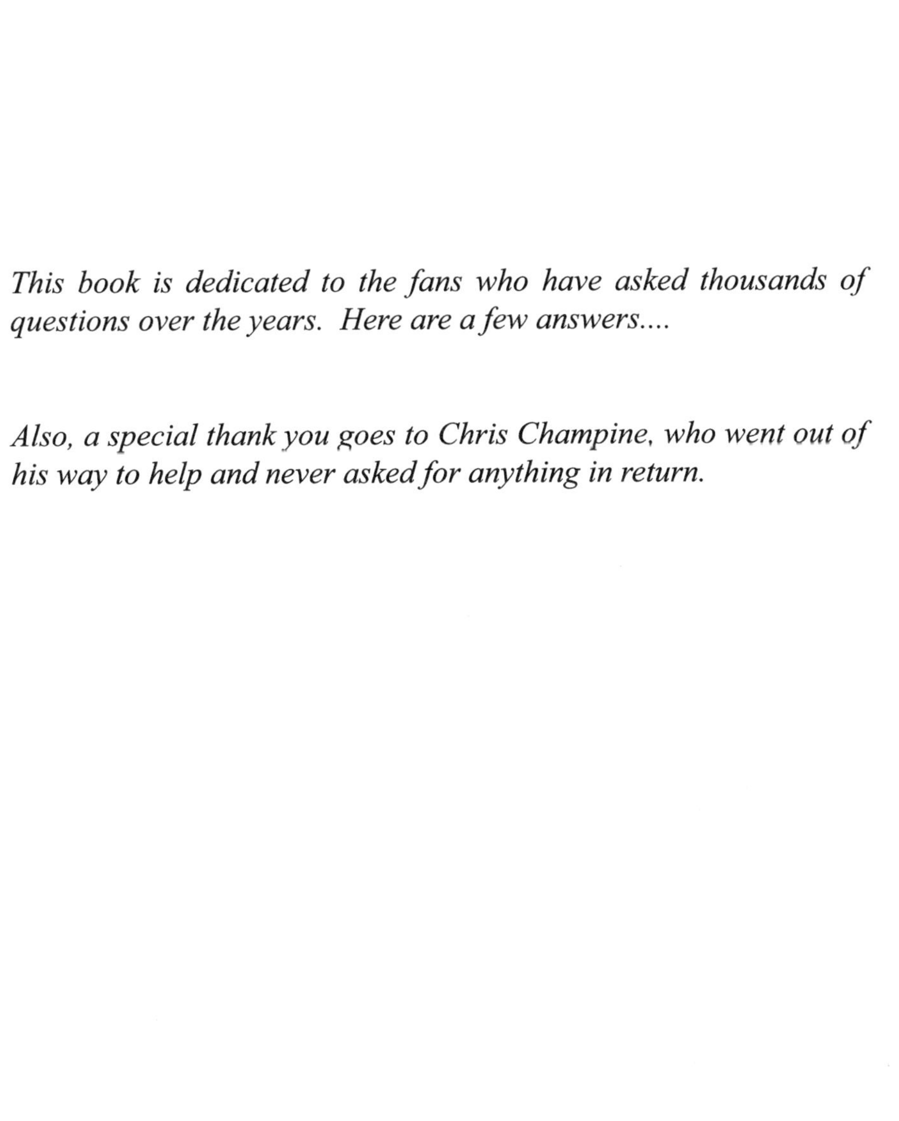

This book is dedicated to the fans who have asked thousands of questions over the years. Here are a few answers....

Also, a special thank you goes to Chris Champine, who went out of his way to help and never asked for anything in return.

TABLE OF CONTENTS

INTRODUCTION: NON-TRIVIAL MATTERS

By Bev Vincent

One day in early January 2004, Brian Freeman e-mailed me to ask if I would be interested in co-editing a Stephen King trivia book. Heck, I'm easy, and the project sounded like fun, so I immediately agreed. Brian's idea was to have Stephen King fans submit the questions. I suggested that we have them send in validation information along with the questions. That way, instead of having to comb through King's collected works and other reference books to confirm the answers to obscure questions, the people submitting the trivia would provide the exact source of their information. We'd sort the questions, verify the answers, edit for style, and fill in any under-represented sections with questions of our own.

The primary source of our questions would be SKEMERs, an on-line group who subscribe to a daily newsletter that combines Stephen King news and discussion with social interaction. Some SKEMERs get together for annual gatherings either in Bangor or at the Stanley Hotel (First trivia question: Inspiration for what Stephen King novel?) in Estes Park. We invited SKEMERs founder and co-president, Michelle Revelle, to write an afterword outlining the group's history, and we committed a percentage of the proceeds to the group, along with an acknowledgement and a free copy of the book to anyone who submitted a question we used in the volume.

Ultimately we opened up submissions to several King fan groups and forums, and we ended up with hundreds and hundreds of questions, with only a few dozen duplicates among them. I had a hundred questions on hand from a trivia contest I wrote for a SKEMERs get-together several years ago and Tyler Hall (The Dark Tower.NET) and Terry Newsom (King's Closet) contributed questions from their trivia contests.

Still, one thing bothered me: How would we make this book different from the two existing volumes of trivia from King expert Steve Spignesi? Brian and I put on our thinking caps and bandied a few ideas back and forth. Our first notion was that we wouldn't sort our questions according to their source. A question wouldn't indicate what novel or story it came from—everything would be jumbled together. If you didn't remember that Joe Camber was a character in *Cujo,* you'd be less likely to know what his wife got him as a present. It was going to be challenging. It was going to be *The Ultimate Stephen King Trivia Book.*

The next evolution in the concept for our book was that we would provide a hints section. Originally, we thought the clues would merely remind the reader of which novel, film or story a question came from, leading him or her gently in the right direction. As time went on, though, I got a little more creative and whimsical. Some hints are puns or contain more trivia themselves. Some are, quite frankly, of no help whatsoever in answering the trivia question, but I hope they'll bring a grin to the corner of your mouth from time to time.

Then Brian suggested having one of my favorite artists, Maine native Glenn Chadbourne, do chapter illustrations. That evolved into the notion of having some questions derived from the illustrations themselves and soon we had our truly unique element: this would be *The Illustrated Stephen King Trivia Book.* Though I think you'll agree that some questions may have even the most well-read King expert scratching his or her head, it's the illustrations that make this volume special. Glenn has a distinctive style that never ceases to amaze me and he turns out his intricate, haunting drawings with amazing rapidity. He soon became our eager collaborator and sent us a quick succession of utterly perfect illustrations.

We hope this book will entertain you and that you'll have a good time going head to head with over a hundred of the biggest Stephen King aficianadoes out there, who have posed over a thousand challenging trivia questions.

A word of warning: the answers to some of these questions might be considered spoilers for books or stories you haven't read. But, then again, you've read them all, haven't you? Some of them two or three times. So that shouldn't be a problem. Just don't say we didn't warn you!

Oh, yes...some of the questions and answers might be considered PG-13. They probably even stray occasionally into R territory. If that sort of thing offends you, we figure you probably aren't reading Stephen King novels in the first place. Caveat lector.

Prefatory matters aside, let's begin. The first chapter contains biographical trivia and is more or less chronological. After that, though, don't expect any rhyme or reason to the order in which you find questions! We've separated them into major categories—and the Dark Tower questions are in somewhat chronological order—but beyond that you're on your own.

Enjoy!

CHAPTER 1
BIOGRAPHY

1 Where was Stephen King born?

a. Bangor
b. Lewiston
c. Portland
d. Castle Rock

2 What is his middle name?

a. Roland
b. Tak
c. Edwin
d. Garrett

3 What were his parents' names?

a. George and Stephanie
b. Donald and Ruth
c. Stephen and Brenda
d. Ralph and Emma

4 What was his father's original last name?

a. King
b. Spansky
c. Klinger
d. Krone

5 After leaving the Merchant Marines, what did his father do for a living?

a. Insurance agent
b. Writer
c. Door-to-door vacuum cleaner salesman
d. Used car dealer

6 What is his brother's name?

a. David
b. Roland
c. Edward
d. Ralph

7 In what year was he born?

a. 1932
b. 1947
c. 1970
d. 1951

8 Besides Maine, in what states did he spend parts of his childhood?

---

a. Hawaii and Alaska
b. New York and Vermont
c. Indiana and Connecticut
d. Pennsylvania and New York

9 In what Indiana town did he once live?

---

a. Muncie
b. Logansport
c. Anderson
d. Fort Wayne

10 According to his biography at *Don't Quit Your Day Job Records*, what Elvis record did King buy in 1956 that ended his relatively quiet childhood?

---

a. All Shook Up
b. Teddy Bear
c. That's All Right Mama
d. Heart Break Hotel

11 Who was the main character in his first original story, written as a child?

---

a. Carrie White
b. Mr. Rabbit Trick
c. Roland of Gilead
d. Captain Trick

12 Who does he call the first paying patron of his stories?

a. His mother
b. His brother
c. His aunt
d. Chris Chesley

13 At the age of eleven, what real-life mass murderer fascinated him?

a. Robert Fellview
b. Charles Manson
c. Ed Gein
d. Charlie Starkweather

14 How many fried eggs did Eula Beulah feed a young Stephen King before locking him in the closet and going to sleep on the couch?

a. 3
b. 5
c. 13
d. 7

15 What was the name of the theater he watched horror movies at while living in Durham, Maine?

a. The Aladdin
c. The Empire
b. The Majestic
d. The Ritz

16 What was the first paper he contributed to?

a. Dave's Rag
b. New Science
c. The Ledger
d. The Drum

17 Who did he collaborate with on *People, Places & Things?*

a. Charles Verrill
b. David King
c. Harlan Ellison
d. Chris Chesley

18 What high school did he attend?

a. Derry
b. Orono
c. Lisbon Falls
d. Pillsbury

19 What was the name of the satire that he published in high school that landed him in detention and almost got him expelled?

a. All the News That's Fit to Spit
b. The Village Vomit
c. The Lisbon Falls Dumb
d. The Vein Tappus

20 What was his first published story?

a. "I Was a Teenage Grave Robber"
b. "Night Surf"
c. "Jerusalem's Lot"
d. "The Woman in the Room"

21 In what year did King make his first professional short story sale?

a. 1967
b. 1969
c. 1968
d. 1970

22 What is his wife's name?

a. Bridget
b. Samantha
c. Tabitha
d. Billie

23 What was his wife's maiden name?

a. Adams
b. Michaels
c. Spruce
d. White

24 In what year did they marry?

a. 1970
b. 1971
c. 1973
d. 1974

25 Where did he first meet his wife?

a. At a book signing
b. At a bar
c. In high school
d. In college

26 Who was the first professor at University of Maine who took an interest in his writing?

a. David Bright
b. Jim Gonis
c. John D. Macdonald
d. Jim Bishop

27 What did his mother want him to get so he'd have something to fall back on?

a. A law degree
b. A medical degree
c. A job at the dry cleaner
d. Teacher's credentials

28 At what school did he teach?

a. Washington Middle School
b. Hampden Academy
c. East Maine High School
d. Camden High School

29 What did King once say he'd rather load crates than do if he had to go back to working a regular job?

a. Work in a laundry
b. Teach High School
c. Work in a mill
d. Drive a transport

30 What field is Tabitha King's degree in?

a. History
b. Political Science
c. English
d. Business

31 Name the King children from oldest to youngest.

a. Joe, Naomi, Owen
b. Owen, Naomi, Philip
c. Naomi, Owen, Philip
d. Naomi, Joe, Owen

32 Stephen King's first published poem was featured in what literary magazine?

a. Moth
b. Clock
c. Everleaf
d. Horizon

33 Who is known as the editor who discovered Stephen King?

a. Chris Chesley
b. Chuck Verrill
c. Kirby McCauley
d. William Thompson

34 What did King buy for his wife at LaVerdier's when he sold *Carrie?*

a. Chocolates
b. Roses
c. A hair dryer
d. Bubble bath

35 How much did the paperback rights to *Carrie* sell for?

a. $1,000
b. $1,000,000
c. $400,000
d. $4,000,000

36 Which of the following has been one of his pseudonyms?

a. Ridley Pearson
b. George Stark
c. John Swithen
d. Paul Sheldon

37 What is the name of his personal publishing company?

a. Castle Rock Books
b. Flagg Press
c. Philtrum Press
d. Bullet Books

38 Tabitha King published her first novel, *Small World,* in what year?

a. 1976
b. 1991
c. 1981
d. 1986

39 Which of the following is not a novel by Tabitha King?

a. *Survivor*
b. *Pearl*
c. *Wolves at the Door*
d. *Rebecca*

40 What magazine selected King as best fiction writer of the year in 1982?

a. Time
b. US
c. The National Enquirer
d. Publishers Weekly

41 How many languages have his novels been translated into?

a. 1-10
b. 11-20
c. 21-30
d. 31-40

42 What is the official name of the ballpark built near his Bangor home?

a. Bangor Baseball Field
b. Stephen King's Field of Dreams
c. Home of Horror Baseball Park
d. Shawn T. Mansfield Stadium

43 When did he leave Viking for a new publisher?

a. 1992
b. 1999
c. 1995
d. 1997

44 What publisher did King choose after leaving Viking?

a. Scribner
b. Random House
c. Knopf
d. Del Rey

45 Under what pseudonym has he published six novels?

a. Dean Koontz
b. Mike Noonan
c. Richard Bachman
d. George Stark

46 Who was the founding editor of the Castle Rock Newsletter?

a. Tabitha King
b. Stephen King
c. Stephanie Spruce
d. Stu Tinker

47 What was the name of his son Owen's baseball team, which he coached?

a. Bangor All Stars
b. Bangor Scream Team
c. Castle Rocks All Stars
d. Bangor West All Stars

48 During what year was he struck by a minivan while walking along the road?

a. 1997
b. 1998
c. 1999
d. 2000

49 According to an interview with *Playboy* magazine, he won't sleep without what?

a. A crucifix
b. Teddy Bear
c. Reading the Bible
d. A light

50 On which of the following pages would he not stop reading a book?

a. Page 19
b. Page 49
c. Page 11
d. Page 99

51 What is the only book published by Philtrum Press not written by King

a. *The Plant*
b. *Six Stories*
c. *The New Lieutenant's Rap*
d. *The Ideal, Genuine Man*

52 What work did he describe as "my oddest experience of selling my wares?"

a. *The Green Mile*
b. *The Plant*
c. The Dark Tower series
d. "Riding the Bullet"

53 The Onion once made a satirical infographic list of reasons for King's retirement. Which of these was one?

a. He wanted to devote more time to scaring his children
b. A clown in his shower drain told him to
c. He wanted to convert his house into a haunted hotel
d. He wanted to fix up his car, Christine

54 According to King, every writer of suspense tales should write at least one story about what?

a. Vampires
b. Worldwide plague
c. A ghostly room at the inn
d. Pets gone bad

55 How many novels has he published?

a. 15-25
b. 25-35
c. 35-45
d. more than 45

56 In an interview with *Playboy* in 1983, what did he say that would make a good epitaph?

a. Writing is felt within your heart not your head
b. I told you I was sick
c. Never forgotten in life or death
d. It is the tale, not he who tells it

CHAPTER 2
NOVELS

1 What is Carrie's last name?

a. King
b. Crabtree
c. Black
d. White

2 Who was the first person to see the woman in Room 217?

a. Delores Vickery
b. Charles Vanderling
c. Mickey Dolan
d. Maude Osgood

3 According to *On Writing*, which novel does King barely remember writing?

a. *Firestarter*
b. *Cujo*
c. *Carrie*
d. *'Salem's Lot*

4 What as-yet unpublished manuscript did King submit for consideration as his second novel?

a. *Sword in the Darkness*
b. *Cannibals*
c. *Flame*
d. *Blaze*

5 The fictional city of Harding in *Sword in the Darkness* is based on what US city?

a. Chicago
b. Detroit
c. New York
d. Knoxville

6 What was Hubert Marsten's wife's name?

a. Birdie
b. Beatrice
c. Lady Bird
d. Bridie

7 What was Patrick Hockstetter's final victim?

a. Mike Hanlon's dog
b. Bill Denbrough's little brother
c. A pigeon
d. His own baby brother

A Name that bull—and the novel depicted above.

8 Eddie Kaspbrak is said to look like which famous actor?

a. Anthony Perkins
b. Jamey Sheridan
c. Jack Nicholson
d. Michael Keaton

9 Tom Gordon played for which baseball team when the book that includes his name in the title was written?

a. New York Yankees
b. Chicago Cubs
c. Boston Red Sox
d. Chicago White Sox

10 Stu Redman thinks he might have filled the gas tank of which dead musician?

a. Jimi Hendrix
b. Jim Morrison
c. Elvis Presley
d. Hank Williams

11 What was the title of Carlos Detweiller's book?

a. *The Plant*
b. *Stand By Me*
c. *True Tales of Demon Infestations*
d. *The Necronomicon*

12 Which of the following was not a folk remedy suggested to Ralph Roberts to cure his insomnia?

a. Whiskey
b. Classical music
c. Honeycomb
d. Exercise

13 Who illustrated the Philtrum Press limited edition of *The Eyes of the Dragon?*

a. Bernie Wrightson
b. Phil Hale
c. Michael Whelan
d. Kenny Ray Linkous

14 Castle Rock Sheriff Alan Pangborn appears in *Needful Things* and what other novel?

a. *Cujo*
b. *The Dark Half*
c. *The Dead Zone*
d. *Misery*

15 What is Eddie Kaspbrak's job as an adult?

a. Architect
b. Limousine driver
c. Deejay
d. Author

16 Carrie has a bad experience on prom night, but what is the event's official title?

a. Homecoming
b. Senior Prom
c. Spring Fling
d. Spring Ball

17 To whom is *'Salem's Lot* dedicated?

a. Naomi Rachel King
b. Tabitha King
c. Douglas Winter
d. Bram Stoker

18 In what county is Derry, Maine?

a. Kenduskeag
b. Haven
c. Penobscot
d. Derry

19 What did Bill Denbrough name his bike?

a. Trigger
b. Bullet
c. Silver
d. Silver Bullet

B An encounter with a crazy police officer begins which novel?

20 Which character says, "Well, then, that's all right, isn't it?"

a. Dolores Claiborne
b. Johanna Noonan
c. Susannah Dean
d. Carrie White

21 Who flattened Jack Torrance's tires?

a. Jack Torrance
b. George Hatfield
c. Al Shockley
d. Delbert Grady

22 A copy of which book was blown up as a potential bomb threat when it was left anonymously at King's Bangor home?

a. *The Stand*
b. *Carrie*
c. *The Girl Who Loved Tom Gordon*
d. *It*

23 Who said, "You can't eat him with his jacket on. Got to get him undressed first."?

a. Mother Abagail
b. Eddie Kaspbrak
c. Louis Creed
d. Randall Flagg

24 Who wrote a poem to Beverly Marsh?

a. Bill Denbrough
b. Mike Hanlon
c. Ben Hanscom
d. Richie Tozier

25 What was the name given to Ralph's group of old timers?

a. Ralph's Rock Bottom Remainders
b. Harris Avenue Old Crocks
c. Bill's Band of Bored Travelers
d. The Old Farts of the Apocalypse

26 Which of these bands played at Carrie's school dance?

a. Jaycee and the Sunbeams
b. Jessie and the Moonbeams
c. Josie and the Moonglows
d. Joselyn and the Marigolds

27 Who published the limited edition of *Insomnia?*

a. Donald M. Grant Publisher
b. Mark V. Ziesing Books
c. Cemetery Dance Publications
d. Philtrum Press

28 What is the name of the dragon in *The Eyes of the Dragon?*

a. Thumper
b. Niner
c. Ringer
d. Trancer

29 According to Mike Noonan, how much of what goes on in a novelist's head is none of the editor's business?

a. 50%
b. 85%
c. 70%
d. 35%

30 What was Jessie Burlingame's maiden name?

a. McMahon
b. Meyer
c. Mahout
d. Manning

31 Who was Pete Riley's roommate?

a. Nate Hoppenstand
b. Ronnie Malenfant
c. Stokely Jones
d. David Dearborne

32 What is Gage Creed's middle name?

a. Louis
b. William
c. Irwin
d. Michael

33 What cellblock was the Green Mile on?

a. B
b. C
c. D
d. E

34 What prestigious award did Johnny Marinville win?

a. Booker Prize
b. Pulitzer Prize
c. Nobel Peace Prize
d. National Book Award

35 The bite of what animal gives Cujo rabies?

a. Bat
b. Raccoon
c. Cat
d. Opossum

36 Who taught Nick Andros to read?

a. Mother Abigail
b. His mother
c. Rudy Sparkman
d. He taught himself

37 How much money did John Smith win from the Wheel of Fortune at the carnival?

a. $300
b. $540
c. $400
d. $1,000

38 Who killed Curtis Wilcox?

a. Dallas Mayr
b. Collie Entragian
c. Atropos
d. Bradley Roach

39 What did Peter and Mary Jackson see on the speed limit sign near Desperation, Nevada?

a. Rabbit
b. Prairie Dog
c. Snake
d. Cat

C There are "little bald doctors" in which novel?

40 What is Speedy Parker's real name?

a. Lester
b. Chester
c. Charles
d. Lloyd

41 Where was the Shop's western compound?

a. Maui
b. San Francisco
c. Seattle
d. San Diego

42 Where is Mike Noonan going when he first spies Kyra Devore?

a. The Sunset Bar
b. McDonald's
c. The Village Cafe
d. K-Mart

43 Which book is not set at least partly in Derry?

a. *It*
b. *The Dead Zone*
c. *Insomnia*
d. *Dreamcatcher*

44 What is the name of the Black Hotel in *The Talisman?*

a. The Agincourt
b. The Alhambra
c. The Kingsland
d. The Kingsford

45 What was Thad Beaumont's father's name?

a. Rick
b. Thad
c. Glen
d. Lester

46 What political position does Danforth 'Buster' Keeton III hold in Castle Rock?

a. On-Call Medical Examiner
b. Head Selectman
c. County Magistrate
d. City Commissioner

47 Where did Answered Prayers open?

a. Junction City
b. Union Junction
c. Union City
d. Uniontown

48 How did Queen Sasha die?

a. A dragon killed her
b. Her food was poisoned
c. Giving birth
d. She got wet lung disease

49 Where does Charles Campion's car crash?

a. Arnette, Texas
b. Los Angeles, California
c. New Orleans, Louisiana
d. Roswell, New Mexico

50 When is Carrie White's birthday?

a. September 21st
b. June 8th
c. December 13th
d. August 19th

51 Route 12 through Cumberland leads to which Maine town?

a. Lewiston
b. Derry
c. Castle Rock
d. 'Salem's Lot

D Abraham Kurtz hunts aliens in Maine in which novel?

52 What is Jack Torrance's full name?

a. Daniel Jack Torrance
b. John Anthony Torrance
c. Jack Daniel Torrance
d. John Daniel Torrance

53 Who is Castle County's On-Call Medical Examiner?

a. Buster Keaton
b. Norris Ridgewick
c. Bob Robertson
d. Ray Van Allen

54 What did Joe Camber's wife give him as a gift?

a. Markson chainsaw
b. Jorgensen chainsaw
c. Jorgen chainfall
d. Black and Decker chainfall

55 What is the name of the prostitute tortured by Norm Daniels?

a. Wendy Yarrow
b. Wendy Parker
c. Cynthia Smith
d. Cindy Yarrow

56 How old was Paul Edgecombe when he started telling his story at Georgia Pines?

a. 94
b. 110
c. 114
d. 104

57 What lasting mark did Ralph Roberts leave on Atropos?

a. He cut off his finger
b. He left a scar on his forehead
c. He cut off his right ear
d. He cut off his left ear

58 At what time did Ruth McCausland blow the clock tower off the Haven Town Hall?

a. 3:05
b. 9:45
c. 5:03
d. 12:00

59 What was the name of Jud Crandall's dog?

a. Cujo
b. Big Pete
c. Rover
d. Spot

60 What was the original title of *The Eyes of the Dragon?*

a. *Kingdom of Delain*
b. *The Napkins*
c. *Needle*
d. *Dragon Eyes*

61 What did Steve Ames see in the aquarium at the Desperation Mining Corp?

a. A human head
b. Fish
c. A human hand
d. Can tah

62 What is the name of the company owned by Maxwell William Devore?

a. MicroAge
b. Visions
c. GraphOs
d. TechnoAge

63 Who killed Wolf?

a. Morgan Sloat
b. Sonny Singer
c. Sunlight Gardner
d. Osmond

64 Which book does not make even a passing reference to Frank Dodd?

a. *It*
b. *Cujo*
c. *The Dead Zone*
d. *Black House*

65 What kind of motorcycle did Johnny Marinville ride?

a. Honda
b. Suzuki
c. Harley
d. Schwinn

66 Where was Eva Miller's boarding house?

a. Derry Street
b. Castle Lane
c. Railroad Street
d. Costello Avenue

67 According to Eddie Jacubois, what is the only diet program where they pay you to participate?

a. Working at the laundry
b. Troop D training program
c. The army
d. Professional football player

68 What was the first Stephen King novel to be adapted as a children's pop-up book?

a. *The Eyes of the Dragon*
b. *The Girl Who Loved Tom Gordon*
c. *Gerald's Game*
d. *The Talisman*

69 How many pins did Vera Donovan insist that Dolores Claiborne use to hang her bed sheets?

a. Eight
b. Four
c. Six
d. Ten

70 Which novel advises, "You can't be careful on a skateboard"?

a. *Dreamcatcher*
b. *Pet Sematary*
c. *The Talisman*
d. *It*

71 What was the name of Roberta Anderson's dog?

a. Buddy
b. Rocky
c. Peter
d. Chewy

E Who is pictured above?

72 Where do Ben Mears and Mark Petrie end up?

a. Los Zapatos, Mexico
b. Xaxchilan, Mexico
c. Zihuatanejo, Mexico
d. Zia Pueblo, Mexico

73 In 1974, King began to write *The House on Value Street,* which ultimately became what novel?

a. *The Stand*
b. *The Dead Zone*
c. *'Salem's Lot*
d. *The Shining*

74 On what date did Zelda Goldman, Rachel Creed's sister die?

a. April 3, 1965
b. April 20, 1965
c. April 8, 1965
d. April 14, 1965

75 How did Nick Andros' mother die?

a. Hit by a car
b. Run over by a truck
c. Hit by a motorcycle
d. Hit by a train

76 What color is the cat on the speed limit sign at the beginning of *Desperation?*

a. White
b. Siamese
c. Black
d. Tiger stripe

77 What is the name of Rose Madder's pony?

a. Ozymandius
b. Radamanthus
c. Minos
d. Sarpedon

78 Who is Tad Trenton's babysitter?

a. Debbie Gehringer
b. Charity Camber
c. Donna Kemp
d. Susan Norton

79 Which breakfast item does Mr. Gray crave?

a. Bacon
b. Eggs
c. Pancakes
d. Maple syrup

80 What did Leigh Cabot almost choke on?

a. Burger King Whopper
b. Sonic Bacon Cheeseburger
c. McDonald's Hamburger
d. White Castle Double Cheeseburger

81 What was the original title of *Dreamcatcher?*

a. *The Talented Mr. Ripley*
b. *Alien*
c. *Ripleys*
d. *Cancer*

82 Who was Gerald Burlingame's partner?

a. Brandon Milheron
b. Branson Mulgrave
c. Pearce Brosname
d. Benjamin Musgrave

83 What was Trashcan Man's real name?

a. Dave Roberts
b. Bobby Terry
c. Donald Merwin Elbert
d. Lloyd Henreid

F Even a blind man could see there's something wrong with the building in this collaborative novel.

84 What is Beverly Marsh's married name?

a. Marsh
b. Grogan
c. Rogan
d. Kersh

85 What was Morgan Sloat's ambition in college?

a. To be a lawyer
b. To be a business financier
c. To be a producer
d. To be a director

86 What did Melinda Moores give to John Coffey the night he came to see her?

a. $50
b. Saint Christopher's medal
c. A lock of her hair
d. The Holy Bible

87 What was the name on the horse racing game box that caught "Buster" Keeton's eye?

a. Win, Place, or Show
b. Trot and Pace
c. Winning Ticket
d. Bet and Wager

88 What was the name of the farmer who gave Charlie and Andy McGee a ride?

a. Marv Stewart
b. Frank Sandford
c. Irv Manders
d. Stuart Anderson

89 Who drives Ralph and Lois to the Derry Civic Center?

a. Ed Deepneau
b. Susan Day
c. Joe Wyzer
d. Dorrance Marstellar

90 Where did Tom Cullen and Nick Andros meet their first survivor of Captain Tripps?

a. Pratt, Kansas
b. Oklahoma City, Oklahoma
c. Kansas City, Kansas
d. Shoyo, Arkansas

91 What was Paul Sheldon's non-genre novel called?

a. *Air Dance*
b. *Misery's Return*
c. *Christine*
d. *Fast Cars*

92 What was the code the officers used to identify a problem relating to Shed B?

a. Code V8
b. Code D
c. Code 29
d. Code B

93 What was Sunlight Gardner's real name?

a. Robert
b. Rodney
c. Richard
d. Randy

94 What business previously occupied the building acquired by Leland Gaunt?

a. H & R Block of Western Maine
b. Western Maine Federal Credit Union
c. Western Maine Realty and Insurance
d. Home Health Care of Western Maine

95 What was missing from George Denbrough upon his death?

a. Yellow slicker
b. His left arm
c. Rain boots
d. His head

96 Where was the excised prologue from *The Shining* first published?

a. *Weird Tales*
b. *Whispers*
c. *Cavalier*
d. *Playboy*

97 What is Duddits' real name?

a. Henry Bowers
b. Douglas Cavell
c. Richie Grenadeau
d. Mr. Gray

98 What graphic imaging software did Max Devore develop?

a. Dot Plot
b. Finger Paint
c. Photo Deluxe
d. Pixel Easel

99 On what date was Ralph Roberts supposed to see "the pin sticker man?"

a. December 6, 1993
b. October 4, 1993
c. May 8, 1993
d. September 6, 1993

100 How many inches of metal does Bobbie Anderson stumble over?

a. 6 inches
b. 12 inches
c. 8 inches
d. 3 inches

101 To what media outlet did Charlie McGee tell her story?

a. *Rolling Stone* magazine
c. ABC News
b. *The New York Times*
d. *People* magazine

102 Who grows up to become perhaps the most promising young architect in America?

a. Ben Hanscom
b. Eddie Kaspbrak
c. Richie Tozier
d. Mike Hanlon

103 What does Trigger Vachon use to write down random bits of information?

a. A receipt
b. Scrap paper
c. A business card
d. A dollar bill

G What is the name of this crow, and what does his name mean?

104 What does C-I-T-Y-L-I-M-I-T spell for Tom Cullen?

a. City Limit
b. Las Vegas
c. Moon
d. Boulder

105 What evil creature was released from the China Pit mine?

a. Tak
b. Entragian
c. Randall Flagg
d. A Low Man

106 "Sugartit" was the colorful epithet used by which character?

a. Dolores Claiborne
b. Trisha McFarland
c. Duddits Cavell
d. Beaver Clarendon

107 What was the name of Morgan Sloat's twinner?

a. Morgan of Orris
b. Sly Sloat
c. Sunlight Gardner
d. Angola Sloat

108 What happened to Mister Dillion?

a. He was shot while chasing a criminal
b. He was "taken" by the Buick during one of its episodes
c. He died of old age
d. He was shot by one of the officers of Troop D

109 According to Arnie Cunningham, who was in for an abysmal fucking at the hands of that all-time rapist, Life?

a. Leigh Cabot
b. Will Darnell
c. Regina Cunningham
d. Buddy Repperton

110 What did Rainbird smoke?

a. Marijuana
b. Marlboros
c. Cuban cigars
d. Home rolled cigarettes

111 Who is Paul Sheldon's editor?

a. Charlie Merrill
b. John Markson
c. Samuel Landry
d. Victor Carune

112 What did Hilly offer to David to get his brother back after a magic act went astray?

a. All his Legos
b. All his G. I. Joes
c. All his Star Wars figures
d. All his marbles

113 Which character shares Tabitha King's birthday?

a. Johnny Smith
b. Annie Wilkes
c. Charlie McGee
d. Wendy Torrance

114 To what author does Mike Noonan compare himself?

a. V.C. Andrews
b. Stephen King
c. John Grisham
d. Tom Clancy

115 What is the name of the hotel where Lily Cavanaugh Sawyer lives with her son?

a. The Agincourt
b. The Alhambra
c. The Kingsland
d. The Kingsford

H What is the name of this clown?

116 What is Brett Camber's mom's name?

a. Charity
b. Caroline
c. Charlotte
d. Cheryl

117 The six installments of *The Plant* are collectively known as what?

a. *Zenith Rising*
b. *Poison Ivy*
c. *True Tales of Demon Infestations*
d. *Day of the Jackal*

118 In which of these books is the protagonist not a writer?

a. *The Dark Half*
b. *Bag of Bones*
c. *Misery*
d. *The Dead Zone*

119 What name is given to the mouse on the Green Mile?

a. Mighty Mouse
b. Knuckles
c. Mr. Jingles
d. Mickey

120 What is the name of Dolores Claiborne's daughter?

a. Amy
b. Selena
c. Charlie
d. Luna

121 What Maine town was the inspiration for Ludlow?

a. Bangor
b. Old Town
c. Orono
d. Orrington

122 What is the name of the drug that Annie Wilkes gives Paul Sheldon?

a. Asril
b. Navril
c. Natril
d. Novril

123 *Gerald's Game* is dedicated to six women with what last name?

a. Willow
b. Spruce
c. King
d. Burlingame

124 Who is Wendy Yarrow's twinner?

a. Dora
b. Drayfus
c. Dorcas
d. Doris

125 What creature brings Tansy Freeneau news of her daughter?

a. A crow
b. A snake
c. A raven
d. A rat

126 What river runs past Castle Rock?

a. Derry
b. Royal
c. Castle
d. Haven

127 What did the cabby think Andy McGee had given him?

a. $1000 bill
b. $100 bill
c. $5000 bill
d. $500 bill

128 What is Johnny Marinville's ex-wife's name?

a. Tania
b. Teresa
c. Tawny
d. Terry

129 Which city does Emil Brodsky originally come from?

a. Daytona Beach, Florida
b. Menlo Park, New Jersey
c. Bangor, Maine
d. Waterloo, Ontario, Canada

130 *Second Coming* was an early name of which novel?

a. *The Tommyknockers*
b. *The Stand*
c. *The Eyes of the Dragon*
d. *'Salem's Lot*

131 What was the name of Danny Torrance's imaginary friend?

a. Ted
b. Tyrone
c. Tony
d. John

132 What did Richie Tozier's father do for a living?

a. He was a dentist
b. He was a general practitioner
c. He was a nurse at Derry Home
d. He was a pharmacist

133 How long was Johnny Smith in a coma?

a. 6 years
b. 2 years
c. 3.5 years
d. 4.5 years

134 Who was the second person to visit Leland Gaunt when he opened?

a. Polly Chalmers
b. Cora Rusk
c. Nettie Cobb
d. Danforth "Buster" Keeton

135 What is written on the cap Mike Noonan buys in Key Largo?

a. DIVE THE KEYS
b. BEACH DUDE
c. GAY PRIDE
d. PARROTHEAD

I What kind of car is pictured?

136 What happened when Jack flipped into Angola, NY?

a. A flash flood
b. An earthquake
c. A hurricane
d. Nothing

137 Who is the main character in George Stark's novels?

a. Thad Beaumont
b. Alexis Machine
c. Richard Bachman
d. Alexis Jackett

138 When Mother Abigail reminisces about a long-ago vacuum cleaner salesman, who is the character named after?

a. The Big Bopper
b. Stephen King's father, Donald
c. Buddy Holly
d. Stephen King's son, Owen

139 What did Bill Denborough's wife do for a living?

a. Actress
b. Cab driver
c. Fashion designer
d. Model

140 Which Daily Bread member tried to kill Ralph Roberts?

a. Sandra McKay
b. Ed Deepneau
c. Charlie Pickering
d. Frank Felton

141 Who was killed during Derry's Canal Days in 1985?

a. Adrian Mellon
b. Don Hagarty
c. Christopher Unwin
d. "Webby" Garton

142 How many times does Rick McCarthy fart before Beaver and Jonesy leave him alone in the bedroom?

a. Once
b. Four times
c. Twice
d. He doesn't fart...he burps.

143 What is the strange, guttural language spoken by Tak?

a. The language of the unformed
b. The language of lost souls
c. The language of todash
d. The language of the lost

144 What fictitious name does Louis Creed use for Victor Pascow in his research paper on the legal ramifications of the treatment of students with VD?

a. Jud Crandall
b. Bango Skank
c. Henry Montez
d. Wendigo Jones

145 What was written on the sign hanging over the counter at the Yellow Submarine?

a. Home of the Yellow Submarine Nightmare
b. Returned Checks: $15
c. No Credit
d. If You Puke, You Pay

146 What was written on Sandra McKay's sweatshirt?

a. Zero to Bitch in Eight Seconds
b. Baby Factory
c. I'm With Stupid
d. Someone Went to Derry and All I Got Was This Stupid Sweatshirt

147 What was the last name of the twins murdered in Trapingus County?

a. Detterick
b. Dietrich
c. Davenport
d. Donahue

J What kind of car is pictured?

148 What is Pie Carver's real name?

a. Karen
b. Katherine
c. Kirsten
d. Kandy

149 In which novel does King quote *The Haunting of Hill House?*

a. *The Shining*
b. *'Salem's Lot*
c. *It*
d. *Bag of Bones*

150 What is engraved on George Stark's gravestone?

a. Not a very nice guy
b. Bye bye, old buddy
c. The sparrows have flown
d. I told you I was sick

151 What is the first item sold by Leland Gaunt to a resident of Castle Rock?

a. A baseball card
b. A pair of Elvis's shades
c. A foxtail
d. An Egyptian amulet

152 What cereal caused so much trouble for Vic Trenton?

a. Cap'n Crunch
b. Rice Krispies
c. Red Razberry Zingers
d. Total

153 What happened to Vicky Tomlinson when she was seven?

a. Her mother died
b. Her parents abandoned her
c. She was in a car accident
d. Her babysitter assaulted her

154 Who was in charge of The Runway 3 Classic?

a. Faye Chapin
b. Don Veazie
c. Jimmy Vandermeer
d. Hamilton Davenport

155 What was the name of Thad Beaumont's newest novel?

a. *The Regulators*
b. *Machine's Way*
c. *The Golden Dog*
d. *Steel Machine*

156 Whose music did Steve Kemp listen to while driving to Portland?

a. Grateful Dead
b. The Ramones
c. AC/DC
d. David Cassidy

157 What novel did SKEMERs vote as their favorite when polled in 2001 by Stephen Spignesi?

a. *The Stand*
b. *The Shining*
c. *It*
d. *The Gunslinger*

158 Which of the following characters is a writer?

a. Carlos Detweiller
b. William Halleck
c. Ted Brautigan
d. Shirley Pasternak

159 Which of the following characters is not a writer?

a. Mike Noonan
b. Dorrance Marstellar
c. Ben Mears
d. Mike Enslin

160 What town is Derry based on?

a. Old Town, Maine
b. Portland, Maine
c. Bangor, Maine
d. Boulder, Colorado

161 On what technicality was the Buick 8 impounded to Shed B?

a. Theft of services
b. Invalid license plates
c. No inspection sticker
d. Abandonment

162 What government project produced the super flu?

a. Arrowhead
b. Project Red
c. Project Blue
d. Lot Six

163 Which book ended with the words "Game Over"?

a. *It*
b. *The Girl Who Loved Tom Gordon*
c. *Gerald's Game*
d. *Firestarter*

164 Where did Harold Lauder hide his ledger?

a. Under a loose brick in the basement
b. Under a stone in the hearth
c. In a shoe box in the closet
d. In a safe

165 Which double-bill movies did Jack and Wolf buy tickets for?

a. *Jaws* and *Cujo*
b. *Sleeping Beauty* and *Cinderella*
c. *The French Connection* and *Chinatown*
d. *Wizards* and *The Lord Of The Rings* cartoons

166 Which of the following was a short story?

a. "Misery's Hobby"
b. "Misery's Quest"
c. "Misery's Return"
d. "Misery's Child"

167 Which of the following is not a little bald doc?

a. Atropos
b. Dorcas
c. Clotho
d. Lachesis

K The sparrows are flying again in which novel?

168 What was Tom Gordon's Red Sox jersey number?

a. 19
b. 36
c. 99
d. 39

169 Which book features Tad Trenton?

a. *It*
b. *Black House*
c. *'Salem's Lot*
d. *Cujo*

170 In what other King work is Dolores Claiborne mentioned?

a. *Needful Things*
b. *The Dead Zone*
c. *Storm of the Century*
d. *The Dark Half*

171 Who won the Monopoly game after the loser's club made the "silver bullets"?

a. Bill
b. Beverly
c. Stan
d. Richie

172 What did Steve Kemp do to the Trenton's bed?

a. Masturbated on it
b. Urinated on it
c. Defecated on it
d. Made it

173 What fictional brand of beer is featured prominantly in *The Talisman* and *Black House?*

a. Nozz-a-la
b. Crimson Lager
c. Kingsland Ale
d. Dark Tower Stout

174 Which book features Bobby Garfield?

a. *It*
b. *'Salem's Lot*
c. *Cujo*
d. *Hearts in Atlantis*

175 From what affliction did Norma Crandall suffer?

a. Diabetes
b. Blindness
c. Arthritis
d. Tuberculosis

176 What did Frannie Goldsmith name her baby?

a. Stuart
b. Peter
c. Jesse
d. Nicholas

177 Which novel was the first King book printed in a signed limited edition?

a. *Christine*
b. *Firestarter*
c. *'Salem's Lot*
d. *The Gunslinger*

178 How much money did Poke and Lloyd get away with in their robbery?

a. $522
b. $1142
c. $63
d. $13

179 Where is the Burlingame cabin located?

a. Little Tall Island
b. Dark Score Lake
c. Haven
d. TR-90

L What is the name of the cabin in this scene?

180 Which of the following wasn't one of Frank Dodd's victims?

a. Alma Frechette
b. Pauline Toothaker
c. Sarah Bracknell
d. Etta Ringgold

181 What is the name of King Roland's dominion?

a. Carfax
b. Delain
c. Alhambra
d. Garlan

182 How does Annie Wilkes permanently maim Paul Sheldon?

a. She smashes his ankle with a sledgehammer
b. She cuts off his foot with an axe
c. She burns his feet with a blowtorch
d. She runs over both legs, crushing them

183 What is Emil Brodsky's army rank?

a. Certified "handy-man"
b. Army Tech Sergeant
c. Private
d. General

184 What did Harold Lauder and the Torrances have in common?

a. Both Harold and Jack Torrance had fathers named Brad
b. Harold and Danny Torrance read Tom Swift books
c. Both Harold and the Torrances drove VW Beetles
d. Both Harold and the Torrances at some point lived on Arapahoe Street in Boulder

185 What kind of car was Christine?

a. 1957 Plymouth Fury
b. 1959 Plymouth Fury
c. 1958 Plymouth Fury
d. 1956 Plymouth Fury

186 Which novel was subtitled: "The LAST Castle Rock Story"?

a. *Cujo*
b. *The Dead Zone*
c. *Needful Things*
d. *The Dark Half*

187 What was Kojak's name before the flu pandemic?

a. Cujo
b. Big Steve
c. Snoopy
d. Big Pete

188 What kind of car did Donna Trenton drive?

a. Ford Mustang
b. Ford Pinto
c. Plymouth Fury
d. Ford Escort

189 On what island does Dolores Claiborne live?

a. Little Tall Island
b. Goat Island
c. Dark Score Island
d. The Reach

190 What was Flagg's pet when he lived in Delain?

a. A raven named Zoltan
b. A baby dragon
c. A billy bumbler
d. A two-headed parrot

191 What kind of car did Richard, Jack and Wolf's brother drive to New Hampshire?

a. Ford Pinto
b. Plymouth Fury
c. Lincoln Continental
d. Cadillac El Dorado

192 Stephen King started writing *It* on September 9, 1981. When did he complete it?

a. December 28, 1985
b. March 2, 1984
c. May 4, 1986
d. April 1, 1982

193 What song was playing when the Army Helicopters attacked the Ripleys?

a. "Werewolves of London"
b. "Sympathy for the Devil"
c. "Don't Fear the Reaper"
d. "Season of the Witch"

194 Who had a vasectomy that self-reversed?

a. Mike Hanlon
b. Richie Tozier
c. Ben Hanscomb
d. Bill Denborough

195 What is Annie Wilkes' mother's name?

a. Cherylia Brondan
b. Crystalla Boydman
c. Crysilda Berryman
d. Crysilla Broughton

196 On what number did John Smith let $54 ride at the Wheel of Fortune?

a. 26
b. 19
c. 13
d. 21

197 What was Joubert's full name?

a. Robert Anthony Joubert
b. Raymond Andrew Joubert
c. Richard Allen Joubert
d. Rodney Albert Joubert

198 What did Ralph and Lois warn the coffee shop waitress about?

a. Little bald men
b. A robbery
c. She had reduced liver function
d. She had cancer

199 What were Payday candy bars changed to in the unabridged version of *The Stand?*

a. Baby Ruth
b. Snickers
c. Almond Joy
d. Milky Way

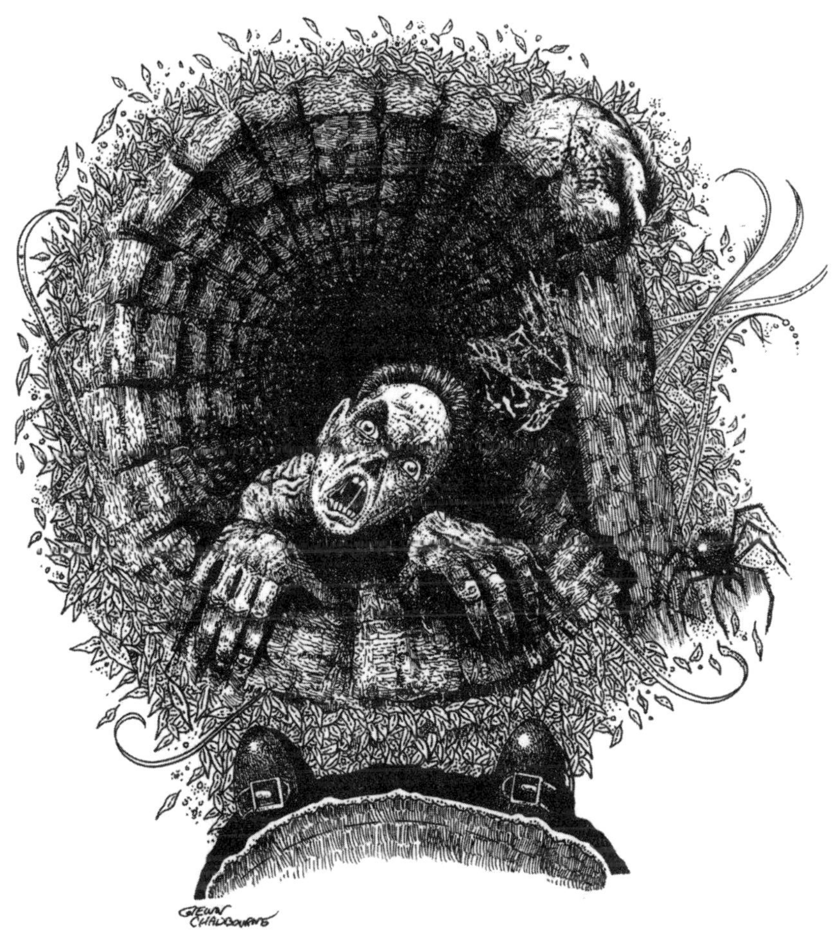

M Who is falling down the well?

200 How many different editions of *From a Buick 8* did Cemetery Dance offer?

a. 0
b. 2
c. 3
d. 1

201 What does Patrick Danville call the figure he paints at the top of the Dark Tower?

a. Randall Flagg
b. The Red King
c. Roland
d. The Crimson King

202 Desperation is in what state?

a. Wyoming
b. Nebraska
c. Montana
d. Nevada

203 What did Flagg poison King Roland's wine with?

a. Dragon Sand
b. Dragon Venom
c. Dragon Tears
d. Dragon Dust

204 Which Red Sox player had his last name misspelled throughout *The Girl Who Loved Tom Gordon?*

a. Jason Varitek
b. Troy O'Leary
c. Nomar Garciaparra
d. Mo Vaughn

205 How old was Georgie Denborough when he met Pennywise?

a. Ten
b. Six
c. Twelve
d. Eight

206 What does "Mi him en tow" mean?

a. "In these silences, something may rise"
b. "Our God is strong, our God is with us"
c. "God is cruel"
d. "Tak is evil"

207 What card game did Bobby Garfield play after leaving the amusement park?

a. Poker
b. Crazy eights
c. Hearts
d. Three card monte

208 Which novel did Jessie Mahout have upside-down whilst eavesdropping on her parents?

a. *The Lion, The Witch and The Wardrobe*
b. *The Hobbit*
c. *Out Of The Silent Planet*
d. *The Eyes of the Dragon*

209 What group performs at the Daughters and Sisters picnic?

a. Queensryche
b. Indigo Girls
c. Styx
d. Crosby, Stills and Nash

210 Who was Phil Sawyer and Morgan Sloat's lawyer?

a. Clint Walker
b. Frank Williams
c. Tommy Woodbine
d. Benny Woodruff

211 Who did Louis Creed refer to as "Oz the Gweat and Tewwible"?

a. Irwin Goldman
b. Jud Crandall
c. Gage Creed
d. Victor Pascow

N What is the name of the man who opened the store known as Needful Things?

212 After the diminishingly small settings of *Misery* and *Gerald's Game,* what did King joke would be the name of the third book in the trilogy?

a. *Closet*
b. *Stool*
c. *Chair*
d. *Sofa*

213 When Johnny Smith "sees" the fire in the nurse's home, what movie was depicted on the poster that was damaged?

a. *Butch Cassidy and the Sundance Kid*
b. *The Shining*
c. *The Magnificent Seven*
d. *Hocus Pocus*

214 What was the first sign the Buick 8 was on its way back to wherever it came from?

a. It started leaking oil
b. The battery went dead
c. A crack appeared in the windshield
d. All four tires went flat

215 On what were the words "Caveat Emptor" written?

a. The front window at Emporium Galorium
b. Leland Gaunt's car
c. A grave marker in the pet sematary
d. A banner at Carrie's prom

216 After what page should the Errata Sheet be included in Grant's Gift Edition of *Desperation?*

a. 12
b. 154
c. 96
d. 453

217 How did war veteran Gary Pervier describe the hippies that started showing up at his place on Town Rd. #3?

a. Long-haired muff divers
b. Crab-crawling assholes
c. Pinko fucksticks
d. All of the above

218 What is the name of the restaurant where the six remaining Losers reunite as adults when arriving in Derry?

a. Jade of the Orient
b. Lucky Garden
c. China Palace
d. Panda Forest

219 Before his father died, where did Jack Sawyer and his parents live?

a. Chicago
b. Los Angeles
c. Miami
d. New York City

220 Where did Andy and Vicky McGee live?

a. Conifer Place
b. Juniper Lane
c. Oakmont Circle
d. Elmwood Estates

221 What do the guards call Mr. Jingles before Delacroix adopts him?

a. Jerry
b. Steamboat Willy
c. Mighty Mouse
d. Mickey Mouse

222 What was the first limited edition to be split into two volumes?

a. *The Stand*
b. *It*
c. *The Talisman*
d. *Wizard and Glass*

223 What politician does Johnny Smith touch and foresee a possible catastrophe?

a. Greg Stillson
b. Ronald Reagan
c. Jimmy Carter
d. George W. Bush

224 When was Annie Wilkes born?

a. All Hallow's Eve
b. April Fool's Day
c. Fourth of July
d. Palm Sunday

225 Which of the following did Johnny Marinville write?

a. *Hammer of the Gods* and *Intensity*
b. *Delight* and *Song of the Hammer*
c. *The Angel of Mercy* and *The Devil in Mrs. Jones*
d. *Open Road* and *Thor's Hammer*

226 Castle Rock is in which state?

a. New York
b. Pennsylvania
c. Maine
d. Colorado

227 What phrase does Lord Malshun use to describe Jack Sawyer?

a. A Short-timer
b. An All-timer
c. A Long-timer
d. Temporarily elevated

228 How did Polly Chalmers kill the spider that escaped the azka?

a. She filled the tub with scalding water
b. She smashed it with a bath towel
c. She stomped on it with her bare foot
d. She squashed it with a plunger

229 Which book features Henry Bowers?

a. *'Salem's Lot*
b. *It*
c. *Different Seasons*
d. *Black House*

230 You Sew and Sew is a store in which novel?

a. *Needful Things*
b. *'Salem's Lot*
c. *The Tommyknockers*
d. *Dolores Claiborne*

231 Which of the following did Ben Mears write?

a. *Being Two*
b. *Steel Machine*
c. *All the Way from the Top*
d. *Conway's Daughter*

0 In which room of the Overlook Hotel does this take place?

232 Which of the following did Mike Noonan write?

a. *Being Two*
b. *Steel Machine*
c. *Air Dance*
d. *Conway's Daughter*

233 How did Frank Dodd's mother die?

a. Shot by Sheriff Bannerman
b. Alzheimer's
c. Stroke
d. Heart attack

234 Who illustrated *Les Yeux du Dragon?*

a. Kenny Ray Linkous
b. David Palladini
c. Christian Heinrich
d. Johann Peterka

235 What book was written for Naomi King and Ben Straub?

a. *Cycle of the Werewolf*
b. *The Dark Half*
c. *The Eyes Of The Dragon*
d. *The Talisman*

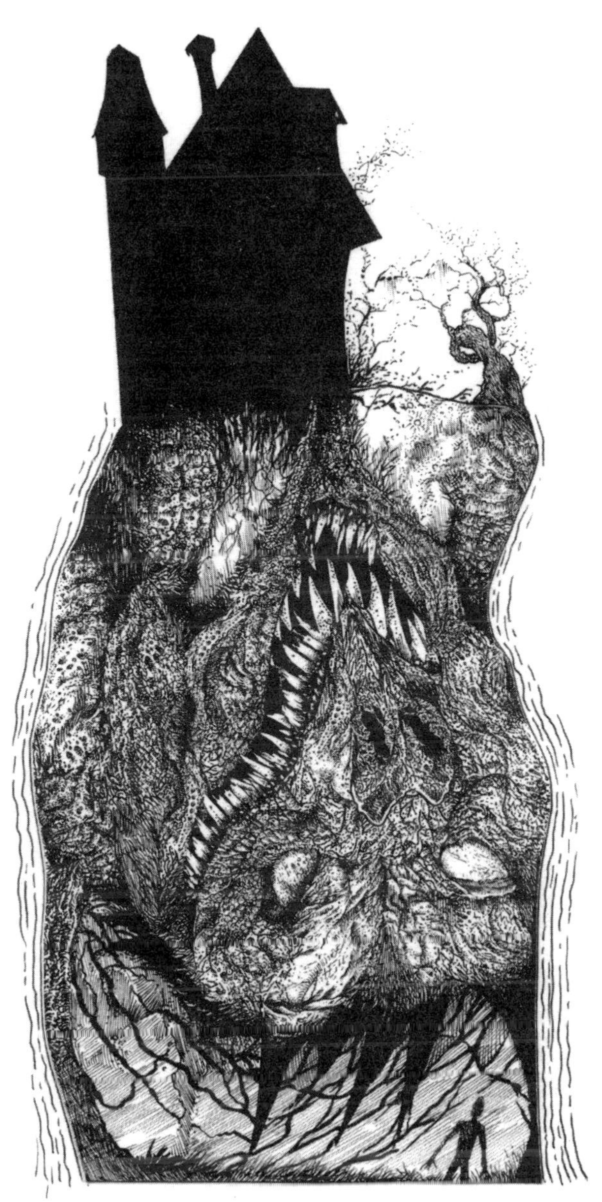

P The road to this house is off which highway?

236 Who was Ralph and Carolyn Roberts' doctor?

a. Dr. McGovern
b. Dr. Creed
c. Dr. Cody
d. Dr. Litchfield

237 What color was the Buick Roadmaster in Shed B?

a. Cherry red
b. Midnight blue
c. Black
d. Blood red

238 What did Mike Ryerson find hanging on the cemetery gates?

a. Goat
b. Cat
c. Dog
d. Danny Glick

239 Which of the following stories does not mention Sheriff Alan Pangborn?

a. *Dolores Claiborne*
b. *The Sun Dog*
c. *The Dark Half*
d. *Needful Things*

240 Who played sax in the Company E Jazz Band?

a. George Brannock
b. Will Hanlon
c. Pop Snopes
d. Dick Hallorann

241 What drug was used on Andy McGee and Vicky Tomlinson?

a. Lot Four
b. Lot Six
c. Project Blue
d. Captain Tripps

242 What was Hal Moores' wife's name?

a. Melba Moore
b. Melly Moores
c. Molly Moores
d. Melinda Moores

243 What was Nadine Cross's pre-flu career?

a. Secretary
b. Journalist
c. Nurse
d. Teacher

244 Which of the following is one of Mike Noonan's ancestors?

a. Jared Devore
b. Sonny Tidwell
c. Harry Auster
d. Scooter Larabee

245 Where did Stuart Ullman spend his winter off?

a. San Diego
b. Fort Lauderdale
c. Miami
d. Key West

246 What kind of truck does Steve Ames drive?

a. U-Haul
b. Ryder
c. Rent-A-Wreck
d. Budget

247 Where did Carrie White's mother work?

a. Blue Ribbon Laundry
b. Dunkin Donuts
c. Wal-Mart
d. Rexall

248 Who was Ralph Roberts' neighbor?

a. Bill McGovern
b. Bob McGovern
c. Bill McGuyver
d. Bill McTeague

249 Who was the father of Fran Goldsmith's child?

a. Jessie Burlingame
b. Harold Lauder
c. Stu Redman
d. Jess Rider

250 Which of the following wasn't one of Patrick Hockstetter's favorite TV shows?

a. Crusader Rabbit
b. Highway Patrol
c. The Outer Limits
d. Science Fiction Theater

251 How much did it cost the Losers to make two silver slugs?

a. A dime
b. One dollar
c. 23 cents
d. Two dollars

252 Who was initially responsible for the spread of the superflu?

a. Victor Champion
b. Vic Trenton
c. Chester Calandar
d. Charlie Campion

253 What did John Tandy's hat say?

a. Derry Landscaping
b. Maine Fertilizer
c. West Side Gardeners
d. Ocean Beach Buccaneers

254 Which of the following isn't a member of the Claiborne family?

a. Joe
b. James
c. Pete
d. Selena

255 In his father's dream, what college did Gage Creed attend?

a. Johns Hopkins
b. Harvard
c. Princeton
d. Yale

256 Which of the following is not mentioned by name in *The Tommyknockers?*

a. Stephen King
b. Peter Straub
c. Bernie Wrightson
d. Greg Stillson

257 What nickname does Speedy give to Jack Sawyer?

a. Jackie
b. Travelin' Jack
c. The Walkin' Dude
d. Jimbo

258 What is the first novel in which a character makes reference to an earlier Stephen King book?

a. *The Shining*
b. *The Dead Zone*
c. *The Stand*
d. *Cujo*

259 What sort of accident did Frannie Goldsmith have as a child that left her all bloody?

a. Fell while roller-skating
b. Struck by a car
c. Fell off a scooter
d. Ran into a mailbox post with her bike

260 What was going to be the setting for the second half of Paul's new Misery book?

a. South America
b. New Zealand
c. Australia
d. Africa

261 Who was Ben Hanscom's high school track coach?

a. Woodsworth
b. Bowers
c. Wilson
d. Woodleigh

262 After Operation Clean Sweep, in which direction does Emil Brodsky lead his troops?

a. West to Pennsylvania
b. South to Florida
c. North to Canada
d. South to Mexico

263 Who spells everything M-O-O-N?

a. Randall Flagg
b. Tom Cullen
c. Duddits Cavell
d. Julie Lawry

Q What is the name of the woman pictured?

264 What was scratched into the desk of the Barker Street Grammar School in Chamberlain?

a. Carrie White eats shit
b. Arnie Cunningham was here
c. Duddits is a Dummy
d. My heart burns there too

265 Whose house resembles a hobbit hole, according to Ralph Roberts?

a. Lois Chasse
b. Bill McGovern
c. Ed Deepnau
d. May Locher

266 What was the date of the 1963 solar eclipse?

a. June 26
b. May 28
c. August 23
d. July 20

267 The Seventh World Fantasy Convention program book contains an excerpt from which novel?

a. *The Talisman*
b. *It*
c. *The Eyes of the Dragon*
d. *The Gunslinger*

268 What did Jack Sawyer become when he grew up?

a. Actor
b. Airline pilot
c. Police lieutenant
d. Insurance salesman

269 Who is Rachel Goldman's husband?

a. James Creed
b. Jack Creed
c. Louis Creed
d. Gage Creed

270 What is the name of the institution where John Coffey is imprisoned?

a. Shawshank Prison
b. Folsom Prison
c. Cold Mountain Prison
d. Green Mile Prison

271 Where did Nick Andros go after his mother died?

a. Children of Jesus Christ Orphanage in Des Moines
b. Children's Home of Des Moines
c. Children of God Orphanage in Des Moines
d. Jesus's Children, an orphanage in Des Moines

272 Which of these four men doesn't make it to Las Vegas?

a. Glen Bates
b. Stu Redman
c. Ralph Brentner
d. Larry Underwood

273 What bank owns the ATM card that Rosie McClendon takes with her?

a. Citibank
b. First Bank Of Maine
c. Mercantile Bank
d. Merchant's Bank

274 What does Dolores Claiborne do with the money she inherits from Vera Donovan?

a. Keeps it
b. Sends her kids to college
c. Gives it to an orphanage anonymously
d. Establishes a scholarship in Vera's name

275 Besides Milo Pressman, who else had a dog named Chopper?

a. Mark Petrie
b. Joe Camber
c. Mike Hanlon
d. Carrie White

276 What's the name of Troop D's mascot?

a. Mister Jones
b. Mister Dillinger
c. Mister Mojo
d. Mister Dillon

277 On the day before the eclipse in 1963, what book was Jessie Mahout's father reading?

a. *Lord of the Flies*
b. *The Holy Bible*
c. *The Innocents*
d. *Profiles in Courage*

278 Who was with Adrian Mellon the night he was killed in Derry?

a. Bob Gray
b. Will Hanlon
c. Don Hagarty
d. Patrick Hockstetter

279 What is the title of Part 5 of *The Green Mile?*

a. "The Mouse On The Mile"
b. "The Bad Death Of Edward Delacroix"
c. "Coffey's Hands"
d. "Night Journey"

280 The signature page of which limited edition might be dated July 5, 1980 or July 8, 1980?

a. *Firestarter*
b. *The Stand*
c. *The Gunslinger*
d. *Dolan's Cadillac*

281 Who wrote the book being read by the person seated next to Beverly Marsh on the flight back to Derry?

a. Robert Ludlum
b. Bill Denborough
c. Ben Mears
d. Mike Noonan

282 Who owned the Oatley Tap?

a. Elder Thayer
b. Smokey Updike
c. Gordon Sloat
d. Inger Stevens

283 Over what period was *Dreamcatcher* written?

a. Sept 16, 1999-May 28, 2000
b. Nov 16, 1999-May 29, 2000
c. Dec 15, 1999-June 29, 2000
d. Oct 13, 1999-April 4, 2000

284 What name does Norman Daniels give to his bull mask?

a. Clay
b. Rosie
c. Ferdinand
d. Ramon

285 What was Louis Creed's profession?

a. Lawyer
b. Mortician
c. Truck driver
d. Doctor

286 Whose voice does Jessie hear after Gerald dies?

a. Gerald's
b. Joubert's
c. Ruth Neary's
d. Prince's

287 What kind of vehicle was Ed Deepnau driving when Ralph witnessed his accident?

a. Toyota
b. Dodge
c. Datsun
d. Honda

288 What was the first of the two movies that Richie, Ben, and Bev saw at the Aladdin Theater before being chased by Henry Bowers and his gang?

a. *The Blob*
b. *I was a Teenage Frankenstein*
c. *I was a Teenage Werewolf*
d. *I Married a Monster From Outer Space*

289 Which of these clever statements did not come from Old Dor?

a. Done bun can't be undone
b. It's a long walk back to Eden, sweetheart, so don't sweat the small stuff
c. Everything I do I rush through so I can do something else
d. Just remember what it's about - nerve. Who has it, and who doesn't

290 What was Stan Uris' wife's name?

a. Patricia
b. Andrea
c. Angela
d. Joan

291 What is the name of the little boy who draws a picture of Roland and the Red King?

a. Peter Donovan
b. Patrick Danville
c. Paul Sheldon
d. Pete Devore

292 Which novel does Stephen King consider a comedy inspired by the Reagan years?

a. *The Tommyknockers*
b. *The Stand*
c. *Needful Things*
d. *The Dark Half*

293 What is Lois Chasse's son's name?

a. Howard
b. Hector
c. Harold
d. Hillary

CHAPTER 3
NOVELLAS

1 How is Ace Merrill related to Pop Merrill?

a. Ace is Pop's father
b. Ace is Pop's nephew
c. Ace is Pop's uncle
d. Ace is Pop's grandson

2 Andy Dufresne is mentioned briefly in what story?

a. "The Body"
b. "The Mist"
c. "Apt Pupil"
d. "Secret Window, Secret Garden"

3 Who illustrated *Cycle of the Werewolf?*

a. Michael Whelan
b. Rick Berry
c. Greg Hildebrandt
d. Berni Wrightson

4 An airplane from which airline was the main setting for "The Langoliers"?

a. American Pride
b. Inside View
c. Jet Yellow
d. United Pride

5 What does 81433-SHNK represent?

a. The license number of the paddy wagon that brought Andy to Shawshank
b. Andy Dufresne's prisoner number
c. The telephone number to Shawshank prison
d. The bank account where Andy hid money

6 Who narrates "The Body"?

a. Vern Tessio
b. Gordie Lachance
c. Dennis Lachance
d. Chris Chambers

7 Whose birthday is September 15th?

a. Kurt Dussander
b. Kevin Delevan
c. Todd Bowden
d. Andy Dufresne

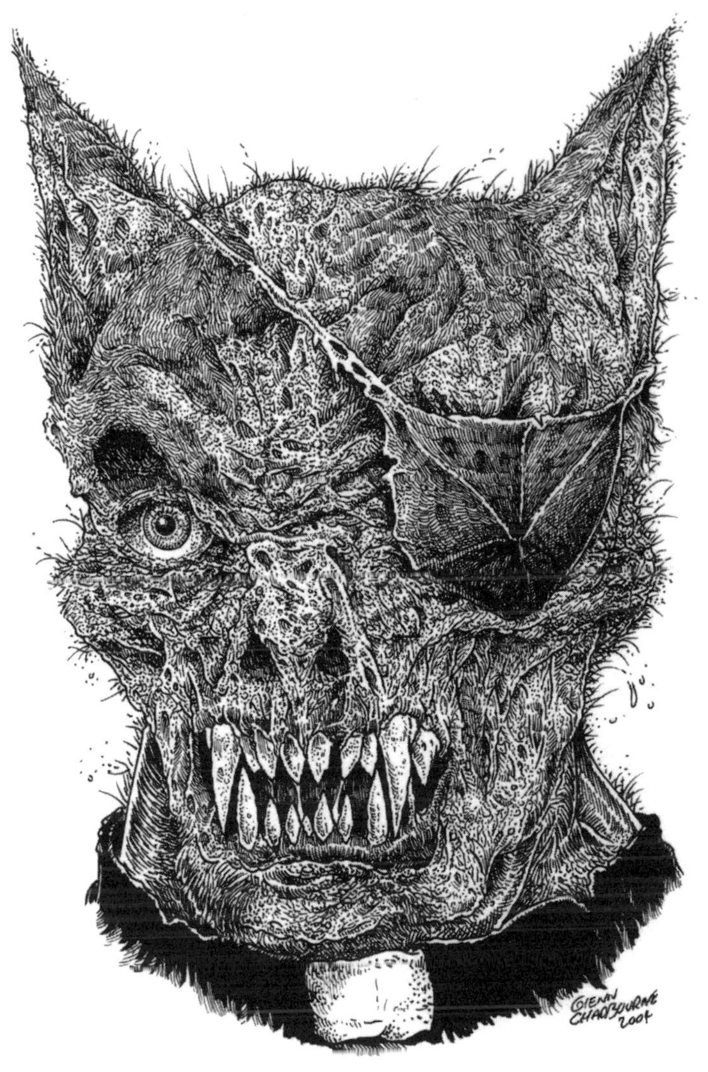

R What kind of creature is pictured above?

8 Which novella was written in a two-week period following the completion of *The Shining?*

a. "The Body"
b. "Rita Hayworth and Shawshank Redemption"
c. "Apt Pupil"
d. "The Breathing Method"

9 Which holiday was canceled in Tarker's Mills for safety reasons?

a. Valentine's Day
b. Thanksgiving
c. Labor Day
d. Fourth of July

10 What town can be reached from Castle Rock via the trestle railroad bridge?

a. Harlow
b. Derry
c. Gates Falls
d. Jerusalem's Lot

11 What did Pop smash up in his back yard?

a. A cuckoo clock
b. A dollhouse
c. A Polaroid Sun 660
d. A birdhouse

12 What was the name of the story that Morton Rainey plagiarized?

a. "Crowfoot Mile"
b. "Secret Window, Secret Garden"
c. "Sowing Season"
d. "The Library Policeman"

13 Who were the two sisters that Pops tried to sell Kevin's camera to?

a. Sara and Nora Oedipus
b. Clotho and Atropos Pustile
c. Eleusippus Deere and Meleusippus Verrill
d. Polly and Nettie Elusippus

14 What is the name of the butler in "The Breathing Method"?

a. Jeeves
b. Roberts
c. Stevens
d. Williams

15 What is Lester Lowe's secret?

a. He is the Tarker's Mills werewolf
b. He killed Andy Dufresne's wife
c. He once owned Kevin's Polaroid
d. His books were overdue at the library

16 Who is the first person killed by a werewolf in Tarker's Mills?

---

a. Stella Randolph
b. Arnie Westrum
c. Alfie Knopfler
d. Brady Kincaid

17 What is the name of the title character in "The Body"?

---

a. Vern Tessio
b. Ray Brower
c. Brian Rusk
d. Todd Bowen

18 In a dream, Kevin Delevan looks for a job in which town where Jack Sawyer was once employed?

---

a. Derry, Maine
b. Oatley, New York
c. Cambridge, Ohio
d. Point Venuti, California

19 What is the fourth and final novella in *Four Past Midnight?*

---

a. "Secret Window, Secret Garden"
c. "Apt Pupil"
b. "The Library Policeman"
d. "The Sun Dog"

S Who drives the car pictured?

20 What is Brady Kincaid doing when the werewolf gets him?

a. Playing soccer
b. Playing basketball
c. Going fishing
d. Flying a kite

21 Which story ended with "And it's *VERY* angry."

a. *Cycle of the Werewolf*
b. "The Library Policeman"
c. "Ballad of the Flexible Bullet"
d. "The Sun Dog"

22 Who is Dave Duncan?

a. The werewolf's second victim
b. The only Newspaper Fairy in Junction City
c. The Tashmore constable
d. Andy Dufresne's business partner

23 Whose story did Morton Rainey plagiarize?

a. Johnny Smith
b. John Kintner
c. John Shooter
d. Johnny Cash

24 Which story was published in a dramatized 3-D sound audio version?

a. "The Mist"
b. "The Breathing Method"
c. "The Body"
d. "Apt Pupil"

25 What is the name of Chris Chambers' eldest brother?

a. John
b. Richard
c. Frank
d. Charlie

26 What science fair project gets Todd Bowden to the state finals?

a. Soil conservation
b. Solar power
c. Air pollution
d. Electricity

27 What was the in-flight movie on American Pride's Flight 29?

a. *Airport*
b. *Airplane*
c. *When Harry Met Sally*
d. *The Godfather*

28 What was Davie Hogan's nickname?

a. Lard Ass
b. Daver
c. Hulk
d. Lard Butt

29 What was Mrs. Andy Dufresne's first name?

a. Linda
b. Mary
c. Susan
d. Amy

30 What book did Ted Brautigan give Bobby Garfield as a late birthday gift?

a. *Lord of the Rings*
b. *Rings Around the Sun*
c. *Lord of the Flies*
d. *Catcher In the Rye*

31 What is located on Angel Street?

a. Andy Dufresne's house
b. The homeless shelter in "The Library Policeman"
c. The club in "The Breathing Method"
d. Mort Rainey's house

32 Whose nickname was Penny?

a. Gordie LaChance
b. Vern Tessio
c. Mort Rainey
d. Brian Engle

33 What was unusual about September and October in Tarker's Mills?

a. The werewolf killed only animals instead of people
b. The werewolf killed more than one person
c. The werewolf did not appear at all
d. The werewolf killed both animals and people

34 "It is the tale, not he who tells it" is the theme for a club in which novella?

a. "Rita Hayworth and Shawshank Redemption"
b. "The Breathing Method"
c. "Secret Window, Secret Garden"
d. "Apt Pupil"

35 How much money did Andy Dufresne leave Red under the stone?

a. Ten $50 bills
b. Fifty $10 bills
c. Twenty $20 bills
d. Twenty $50 bills

36 What was notable about the way the Library Policeman spoke?

a. He stuttered
b. He had a lisp
c. He had a German accent
d. He had a Maine accent

37 What kind of camera did Todd use to take pictures of Dussander?

a. Polaroid
b. Nikon
c. Hasselbad
d. Kodak

38 What book does Ted use to illustrate the "definition of a tragedy"?

a. *Lord of the Flies*
b. *Catcher in the Rye*
c. *The Inheritors*
d. *Oedipus Rex*

39 Who told the story called "The Breathing Method"?

a. George Waterhouse
b. Peter Andrews
c. David Stevens
d. Emlyn McCarron

T Kevin Delevan and his birthday gift are the focus of his novella.

40 When is the werewolf killed in *Cycle of the Werewolf?*

a. Halloween
b. Christmas Eve
c. New Year's Eve
d. Valentine's Day

41 Which of the following is a Low Man?

a. Tak
b. Cam
c. Munshun
d. Atropos

42 Which of the following stories contains two other King stories?

a. "The Sun Dog"
b. "The Mist"
c. "Low Men in Yellow Coats"
d. "The Body"

43 What is Andy Dufresne's destination after he escapes from prison?

a. Zihuatanejo
b. Los Zapatos
c. Xaxchilan
d. Zia Pueblo

44 Who is the first woman mentioned by name in *Hearts In Atlantis?*

a. Liz Garfield
b. Nancy Drew
c. Dorothy McGuire
d. Carol Gerber

45 What did Dussander drink from a coffee mug?

a. Coffee
b. Bourbon
c. Milk
d. Tea

46 "You stole my story" is the opening line to which novella?

a. "The Library Policeman"
b. "The Sun Dog"
c. "The Langoliers"
d. "Secret Window, Secret Garden"

47 Whose poster did Andy have up in his cell when he escaped?

a. Rita Hayworth
b. Linda Ronstadt
c. Farrah Fawcett
d. Stevie Nicks

48 What state did the main character in "The Breathing Method" come from?

a. Wisconsin
b. Washington
c. Montana
d. North Dakota

49 During which month did Brady Kincaid meet his unfortunate death?

a. June
b. April
c. March
d. May

50 Which of the following posters did not hang in Andy's cell?

a. Hazel Court
b. Farrah Fawcett
c. Marilyn Monroe
d. Jayne Mansfield

51 How are the chapters designated in *Cycle of the Werewolf?*

a. Roman numerals
b. Name of the character who dies
c. Phases of the moon
d. Months of the year

U Flight 29 ends up in a vacated world in which novella?

52 According to Ted Brautigan, what doesn't "give up all their secrets at once?"

a. Adults
b. Books
c. Low men
d. Politicians

53 What was written on the sign in the Junction City library?

a. SILENCE IS GOLDEN
b. PLEASE TRY TO BE QUIET
c. SILENCE!
d. QUIET, PLEASE!

54 Where does Marty Coslaw live?

a. Castle Rock
b. Harlan
c. Tarker's Mills
d. Derry

55 *Everybody Drops the Dime* is the title of a collection by which fictitious author?

a. John Kintner
b. Morton Rainey
c. Mike Noonan
d. John Shooter

56 What is Richard Sifkitz's primary medical problem

a. Bum knee
b. Heart murmur
c. High cholesterol
d. Incontinence

57 Which of the following is not a section of "Stationary Bike?"

a. "Metabolic Workmen"
b. "On the Road to Herkimer"
c. "Man With Shotgun"
d. "Answering the Call"

58 Who is Barry Casselman?

a. Richard Sifkitz's agent
b. Mort Rainey's agent
c. Gordie Lachance's agent
d. Stephen King's agent

CHAPTER 4
SHORT STORIES

1 How often does it rain toads in Willow, Maine?

a. Every 3 years
b. Every 5 years
c. Every 7 years
d. Every 9 years

2 Where did the 7" hunting knife found in Carl Amalara's footlocker come from?

a. Kittery Trading Post
b. L. L. Bean
c. Cabela's
d. Wal-Mart

3 In *Six Stories,* the title page preceding each story had Stephen King's name listed above the story title for all but one of the stories. For which story did King's name appear *below* the title?

a. "Autopsy Room Four"
b. "L.T.'s Theory of Pets"
c. "Lunch at Gotham Café"
d. "Luckey Quarter"

4 What kind of car takes Deke, Randy, LaVerne and Rachel from Horlicks University to Cascade Lake?

a. Trans Am
b. Firebird
c. Camaro
d. Corvette

5 In what city is Horlicks University located?

a. Knoxville
b. Detroit
c. New York
d. Pittsburgh

6 Which of the following stories features Horlicks University?

a. "The Crate"
b. "You Know They've Got a Hell of a Band"
c. "One for the Road"
d. "The Ballad of the Flexible Bullet"

V In which short story does the sky rain killer toads?

7 What was the setting for a story first published in *USA Weekend* magazine in 1995?

---

a. Las Vegas, NV
b. Carson City, NV
c. Reno, NV
d. Atlantic City, NJ

8 Who inherited Uncle Otto's money?

---

a. University of Maine Forestry Dept.
b. Billy Dodd
c. Horlicks University
d. New England Paper Co.

9 In what infamous town did Richard Kinnell live?

---

a. Castle Rock
b. Haven
c. Derry
d. Boulder

10 What were the make, model, and tail designation of Dwight Renfield's plane?

---

a. Beechcraft Eagle N471B
b. Lear Titanium B50512
c. Piper Cub L47CJ
d. Cessna Skymaster 337 N101BL

11 Before he went to medical school, what did Richard Pine admit to doing?

a. Killing his father
b. Changing his name
c. Tasting human flesh
d. Hitting a pedestrian with his car

12 How many stories in *Everything's Eventual* were previously unpublished?

a. 0
b. 1
c. 2
d. 3

13 "Dolan's Cadillac" was first serialized in what publication?

a. SKIN
b. Ubris
c. Castle Rock Newsletter
d. The Magazine of Fantasy and Science Fiction

14 Which of the following stories was published as a screenplay?

a. "Dedication"
b. "Sneakers"
c. "Head Down"
d. "Sorry, Right Number"

15 During what month do four teenagers go swimming in Cascade Lake?

a. January
b. July
c. October
d. April

16 How was Ophelia Todd's husband killed?

a. Cut up in an industrial fan
b. In a car accident
c. In a freak earthquake
d. By a walking windmill

17 How did John Dillinger and Homer Van Meter disguise Jack Hamilton's body?

a. They poured lye on his face and fingers
b. They burned his body
c. They cut his body up into pieces
d. They blew his body up with a stick of dynamite

18 What is the name of the main character in "Sneakers"?

a. William Tell
b. Penn Teller
c. John Tell
d. John Smith

19 "Squad D" was written for which unpublished anthology?

a. *Dark Harvest*
b. *October Dreams*
c. *Last Dangerous Visions*
d. *Borderlands 2*

20 Who was supposed to edit the unpublished anthology in which "Squad D" would have appeared?

a. Peter Straub
b. Bill Thompson
c. Ramsey Campbell
d. Harlan Ellison

21 Where was "The Revelations of 'Becka Paulson" first published?

a. *Maine*
b. *Cavalier*
c. *The Magazine of Fantasy and Science Fiction*
d. *Rolling Stone*

22 Where else has "The Revelations of 'Becka Paulson" seen print?

a. *Night Shift,* Doubleday
b. *Skeleton Crew,* Scream Press
c. *Nightmares and Dreamscapes,* Viking
d. *Everything's Eventual,* Scribner

23 Which of the following is not in *Night Shift?*

a. "I Am the Doorway"
b. "Night Surf"
c. "The Woman in the Room"
d. "My Pretty Pony"

24 What part of the hitchhiker did the chattery teeth attack first?

a. Neck
b. Nose
c. Fingers
d. Groin

25 In which state would you find Rock and Roll Heaven?

a. Nevada
b. Maine
c. Oregon
d. Massachusetts

26 Which story has only been published in the NECON XX Commemorative Volume?

a. "The Old Dude's Ticker"
b. "The Tale of Grey Dick"
c. "The Dreaded X"
d. "The New Lieutenant's Rap"

27 Who was King's co-author for the story in the previous question?

a. Peter Straub
b. Joe King
c. Richard Bachman
d. Edgar Allan Poe

28 What did Alfie Zimmer sell?

a. Gourmet foods
b. Amway products
c. Vacuum cleaners
d. Bibles

29 What shampoo brand did David Drayton draw ads for while waiting for his career as an artist to take off?

a. Breck
b. Prell
c. Golden Girl
d. Johnson & Johnson

30 Which story does not appear in *Six Stories?*

a. "Luckey Quarter"
b. "Blind Willie"
c. "Stationary Bike"
d. "Autopsy Room Four"

31 "The Cat from Hell" was first published where?

a. *Magicats*
b. *Cavalier*
c. *Twist of the Tale*
d. *Tales from the Darkside*

32 What kind of snake bit Howard Cottrell?

a. African Boomslang
b. Peruvian Boomslang
c. Mexican Boomslang
d. Indonesian Boomslang

33 Springheel Jack was the nickname of a serial killer in which story?

a. "Rainy Season"
b. "Strawberry Spring"
c. "The Night Flier"
d. "In the Deathroom"

34 Which T.V. show influenced King to write "Autopsy Room Four"?

a. Alfred Hitchcock Presents
b. The Twilight Zone
c. The Outer Limits
d. Night Gallery

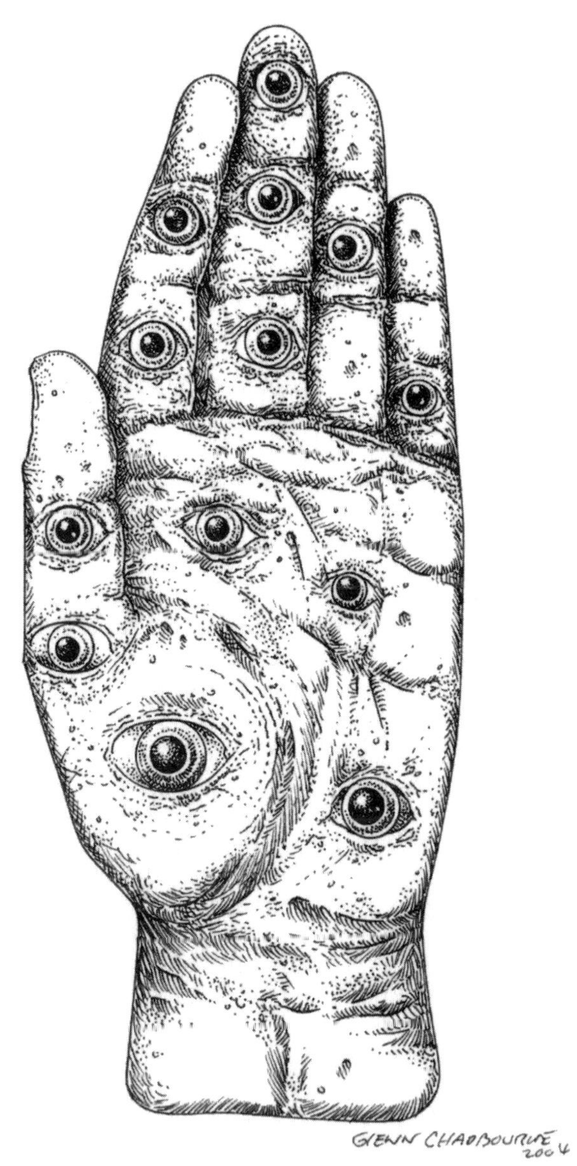

W Which short story features strange changes to a character's hands?

35 Which story was a precursor to *The Stand?*

a. "The Mist"
b. "The Rainy Season"
c. "The Reach"
d. "Night Surf"

36 Who is King's co-author in the collection of eighteen one-page science fiction and horror short stories that make up *People, Places & Things?*

a. Bill Thompson
b. Chris Chesley
c. David King
d. Kirby McCauley

37 What short story takes place in a haunted hotel room?

a. "1020"
b. "1260"
c. "1408"
d. "1458"

38 What city was the setting for "The Ten O'Clock People"?

a. Dallas
b. Boston
c. Pittsburgh
d. New York

39 What King novella will be published in *Crimes*, edited by Ed McBain?

a. "Derry, The Untold Story"
b. "The Things They Left Behind"
c. "Crossing the Green Monster"
d. "Evolution of the Crimson King"

40 In what year did David Drayton's father first fly the American flag over their boathouse?

a. 1928
b. 1943
c. 1935
d. 1936

41 What breed of dog was purchased by Lulubelle as an anniversary gift for her husband?

a. Miniature Doberman pinscher
b. St. Bernard
c. Schnauzer
d. Jack Russell Terrier

42 In which magazines did King publish short stories during 2003?

a. *Playboy* and *The New Yorker*
b. *Cemetery Dance* and *Esquire*
c. *The New Yorker* and *Esquire*
d. *Cemetery Dance* and *Fangoria*

43 What days did Dr. Harper suggest for appointments with Lester Billings?

a. Tuesdays and Thursdays
b. Wednesdays and Fridays
c. Mondays and Fridays
d. Mondays and Tuesdays

44 What unpublished story was the first attempt at what became *The Green Mile?*

a. "The Last Twenty Steps"
b. "Walking the Mile"
c. "What Tricks Your Eye"
d. "The Mouse on the Mile"

45 What is the destination for Jaunt-701?

a. Whitehead City, Mars
b. New York's Port Authority Terminal
c. Alpha Centauri
d. Moonbase Alpha

46 What does the tattoo on Bryan Adam's bicep read?

a. LED ZEP RULE
b. KISS ARMY
c. AC/DC ROCK
d. DEF LEPPARD 4-EVER

47 Which of the following four teenagers dies first?

a. Laverne
b. Rachel
c. Randy
d. Deke

48 How many times did Cressner say he proposed his wager to people before Stan Norris?

a. 6 times
b. 12 times
c. 8 times
d. 4 times

49 Complete this phrase: I ____ The Bullet At Thrill Village, Laconia.

a. Dodged
b. Shot
c. Ate
d. Rode

50 What movie star does Lulubelle remind her husband of?

a. Demi Moore
b. Kathy Bates
c. Liza Minelli
d. Lucille Ball

51 How much money did King receive for his first fiction sale to *Startling Mystery Stories?*

a. $127
b. $50
c. $35
d. $100

52 What is the name of the woman who says, "The moving finger has writ, not in fire, but in lines of mist."

a. Mrs. Carmody
b. Mrs. Carmichael
c. Mrs. Carruthers
d. Mrs. Drayton

53 Dick Morrison was charged $5000.50. What was the 50 cents for?

a. Sales tax
b. Electricity
c. Dry cleaning
d. Matches

54 What medication does Johnny give to the woman in room 312?

a. Darvon
b. Anacin
c. Keflex
d. Morphine

X A picture purchased at a yard sale becomes the source of a writer's doom in which short story?

55 What is Mrs. Todd's first name?

a. Tabitha
b. Mildred
c. Ophelia
d. Desdemona

56 Under what name did Stephen King originally publish "The Fifth Quarter"?

a. Richard Bachman
b. Dean Koontz
c. Stephen King
d. Jonathan Swithen

57 At which hotel is Martha Rosewall the Chief Housekeeper?

a. Alhambra
b. Le Palais
c. Savoy
d. Ritz

58 "Children of the Corn" first appeared in what popular men's magazine?

a. *Playboy*
b. *Dude*
c. *Juggs*
d. *Penthouse*

59 What does Richard Kinnell buy at a yard sale?

a. A rare book
b. An umbrella
c. Dishes
d. A painting

60 Which collection includes the short stories "Battleground" and "The Ledge"

a. *Skeleton Crew*
b. *Everything's Eventual*
c. *Night Shift*
d. *Nightmares and Dreamscapes*

61 What is Brent Norton's occupation?

a. Doctor
b. Lawyer
c. Car salesman
d. Teacher

62 The phrase "Fun Is Fun and Done Is Done" is from which short story?

a. "The Road Virus Heads North"
b. "Riding The Bullet"
c. "Everything's Eventual"
d. "Luckey Quarter"

63 What reward will Jhonathan receive for killing the three witches?

a. The princess' hand in marriage
b. He will be knighted
c. His father will be set free from the dungeon
d. 5000 crowns

64 How many stories are in *Everything's Eventual?*

a. Fifteen
b. Fourteen
c. Thirteen
d. Twelve

65 Which short story was included as part of F13?

a. "Everything's Eventual"
b. "The Old Dude's Ticker"
c. "Riding the Bullet"
d. "The New Lieutenant's Rap"

66 What was the original title of the story Stephen King sold to *Adam Magazine* in 1969 and then rewrote from memory in 1981 during the shooting of *Creepshow?*

a. "The Float"
b. "The Ballad of the Flexible Bullet"
c. "The Reach"
d. "The Mist"

67 What is written on a napkin on the dust jacket spine of *Everything's Eventual?*

a. Oh Lord please help us
b. Oh God please help us.
c. Oh no please help us
d. oh man please help us

68 What did Dudley suggest Brandon Pearson do so he would not faint?

a. Count backwards from 100
b. Say the alphabet
c. Start naming states
d. Sing Beatles songs

69 Who lives in Reg Thorpe's typewriter?

a. Fornus
b. Frodo
c. Bellis
d. Fornix

70 What character comes from Little Tall Island?

a. Maddie Pace
b. Elsie Graham
c. Katie Widerman
d. Melissa Bradbury

71 In what state do Vicky and Burt Robeson get lost?

a. Kansas
b. Wyoming
c. Utah
d. Nebraska

72 Near what town is Jordy Verrill's farm located?

a. Cleaves Mills, New Hampshire
b. Cleaves Mills, Maine
c. Castle Rock, Maine
d. Castle Rock, New Hampshire

73 Which volume in the *Borderlands* anthology series contains a Stephen King story?

a. *Borderlands 1*
b. *Borderlands 3*
c. *Borderlands 5*
d. *Borderlands 2*

74 What was the name of the nasty little boy who loves to torture animals in the one-page story "The Thing Under The Well"?

a. Arnie Cunningham
b. Oglethorpe Crater
c. Butch McCutcheon
d. Ronny Devlin

75 What was the name of the diner where a Reo hits Snodgrass?

a. The Dixie Boy
b. Bubba's Diner
c. Conant's Truck Stop
d. Bill's Truck Stop

76 After questioning the morality of his job, Dinky Earnshaw decided that he didn't give:

a. A fuck.
b. A fuck in a rabbit hutch.
c. A fuck at a rolling donut.
d. A righteous fuck.

77 What two early King short stories recently turned up in old copies of his high school newspaper, The Drum?

a. "The King Family and the Wicked Witch" and "Jumper"
b. "Jumper "and "Rush Call"
c. "The 43rd Dream" and "Code Name: Mousetrap"
d. "The Glass Floor" and "The Reaper's Image"

78 According to *The Complete Guide to the Works of Stephen King,* "The Killer" was a rewrite of what story in *People, Places, and Things?*

a. "The Hotel at the End of the Road"
b. "The Star Invaders"
c. "I've Got to Get Away!"
d. "The Stranger"

79 What town is the setting for "Gramma"?

a. Derry
b. Cleaves Mills
c. Ludlow
d. Castle Rock

80 What *Inside View* reporter goes in search of a vampire?

a. Ricky Dee
b. Randy Dye
c. Richard Dees
d. Robert Dove

81 Which issue of *Cemetery Dance* magazine contains a King short story?

a. Issue #2
b. Issue #13
c. Issue #14
d. Issue #25

82 In what collection does the phrase "Do you love?" become a continuing theme?

a. *Night Shift*
b. *Skeleton Crew*
c. *Four Past Midnight*
d. *Nightmares and Dreamscapes*

Y Trucks come alive in which short story?

83 What were the three stories on the audiobook *Blood and Smoke?*

a. "In the Deathroom", "1408", "Luckey Quarter"
b. "1408", "In the Deathroom", "Lunch at the Gotham Café"
c. "Lunch at the Gotham Café", "In the Deathroom", "Riding the Bullet"
d. "In the Deathroom", "1408", "The Death of Jack Hamilton"

84 Which famous musician does Clark Willingham not meet in Rock and Roll Heaven?

a. Buddy Holly
b. Elvis
c. Kurt Cobain
d. Janis Joplin

85 What King story appears in *Borderlands 5?*

a. "The Things They Left Behind"
b. "Stationary Bike"
c. "Answering the Call"
d. "One of Those Weeks"

86 "The Reach" was originally published under what title?

a. "Luckey Quarter"
b. "The Long Walk"
c. "Home Delivery"
d. "Do the Dead Sing?"

87 Which of these stories features a man contemplating suicide?

a. "In the Deathroom"
b. "1408"
c. "The Death of Jack Hamilton"
d. "All That You Love Will Be Carried Away"

88 Besides water, what's in the glass on the cover of *Everything's Eventual?*

a. A diamond
b. A drop of blood
c. A dime
d. Ice cubes

89 What will happen if Jhonathan does not kill the three witches?

a. He will be beheaded
b. His parents will be locked in the dungeon
c. He will be banished from the kingdom
d. A curse will befall the kingdom

90 Which of Brent Norton's cars got destroyed during the storm?

a. Thunderbird
b. Mercedes
c. Saab
d. Jaguar

91 When King is asked to read a story out loud, which one does he prefer?

a. "The Man in the Black Suit"
b. "1408"
c. "Riding the Bullet"
d. "L.T.'s Theory of Pets"

92 "The Revelations of 'Becka Paulson" became part of which novel?

a. *Gerald's Game*
b. *The Tommyknockers*
c. *Needful Things*
d. *Dolores Claiborne*

93 Which character in "Why We're in Vietnam" is named for a real person who won the chance to appear in a King story at a Bangor Symphony Orchestra fundraising auction?

a. Hugh Brennan
b. Sally McBride
c. Mary Theresa Charlton
d. Denny Rivers

94 What is the first story in *Nightmares and Dreamscapes?*

a. "The Mist"
b. "Dolan's Cadillac"
c. "The End of the Whole Mess"
d. "Rainy Season"

95 What was the nickname of the serial killer stalking Ames, Iowa?

a. Springheel Jack
b. The Switchblade Man
c. The Axe Man
d. The Hatchett Man

96 Complete this story title: "The Man in the ____ Suit".

a. Ice-cream colored
b. Blue
c. Dirty
d. Black

97 Which story features the entire King family?

a. "Nona"
b. "Mrs. Todd's Shortcut"
c. "The Leprechan"
d. "The King Family and the Wicked Witch"

98 What nickname did Lulubelle give her husband?

a. Maple duff
b. Sugar buns
c. Hunny bunny
d. Sweetums

99 What government project is located in Shaymore?

a. Project Blue
b. Arrowhead
c. The Shop
d. Milestone

100 What does Reg Thorpe write at the end of each letter to Henry Wilson?

a. Nil Satis Nisi Optimon
b. Fornit Some Fornus
c. Cogito Ergo Sum
d. Veni Vidi Vici

101 What island is the setting for "The Reach"?

a. Little Tall Island
b. Goat Island
c. Fantasy Island
d. Raccoon Head

102 Which Federal Foods Supermarket manager shares his name with a character from Ed McBain's 87th Precinct novels?

a. Bud Brown
b. Meyer Meyer
c. David Drayton
d. Ollie Weeks

Z Rats inhabit the basement in which short story?

103 Finish this story title: "The Road Virus Heads ____."

a. East
b. North
c. West
d. South

104 Which King short story did not first appear in *Night Visions V?*

a. "The Reploids"
b. "Harvey's Dream"
c. "Sneakers"
d. "Dedication"

105 Which short story collection was published first?

a. *Everything's Eventual*
b. *Night Shift*
c. *Nightmares and Dreamscapes*
d. *Skeleton Crew*

106 What award did King win in 1996 for *The Man In The Black Suit?*

a. Hugo
b. O. Henry
c. Bram Stoker
d. Pulitzer

107 What does "Jerusalem's Lot" have in common with *Dracula?*

a. Both stories feature vampires
b. Dwight Renfield is a character in both
c. Both take place in England, at least in part
d. Both are told in epistolary form

108 The mill in "Graveyard Shift" is located in the same town as what other King story?

a. "Cycle of the Werewolf"
b. "The Ballad of the Flexible Bullet"
c. *Kingdom Hospital*
d. "Rita Hayworth and Shawshank Redemption"

109 What Rolling Stones song is mentioned in "Night Surf"?

a. "Angie"
b. "Sympathy for the Devil"
c. "Satisfaction"
d. "Emotional Rescue"

110 Where did Adelle Frawley die?

a. On the beach
b. In the Blue Ribbon Laundry
c. In 'Salem's Lot
d. In her apartment

111 Where does "Gray Matter" take place?

a. Derry
b. Castle Rock
c. Portland
d. Bangor

112 What is John Renshaw's minimum fee?

a. $10,000
b. $5,000
c. $50,000
d. $2,500

113 Where does Jim Norman teach?

a. Hampden Academy
b. Harold Davis High School
c. Derry High School
d. University of Maine

114 What happened to Harold Parkette's lawnmower?

a. Busted blade
b. He ran over a cat with it
c. Gummed up spark plug
d. Wouldn't start

115 Edward Jackson Hamner knew what Elizabeth needed. What did she need first?

a. Strawberry double-dip cone
b. $2000 for tuition
c. For Tony to die
d. Airfare to visit her parents

116 Which of the following stories takes place in Hemingford Home, home to Mother Abigail?

a. "I Know What You Need"
b. "Strawberry Spring"
c. "The Last Rung on the Ladder"
d. "The Lawnmower Man"

117 Which of the following did not teach at Acorn Street Grammar School?

a. Mr. Norman
b. Miss Kinney
c. Mrs. Trask
d. Miss Bird

118 Where did Dennis Shelburn find the monkey?

a. Caught it while fishing
b. In a box in the attic
c. In a box in the basement
d. In his father's closet

119 Which story features a character nicknamed The Beaver?

a. "Here There Be Tygers"
b. "The Mist"
c. "The Monkey"
d. "Cain Rose Up"

120 What kind of car did Ophelia Todd drive?

a. Mercedes
b. BMW
c. Plymouth Fury
d. Pinto

121 "If you want to skip the turnpike . . . you'd go to Mechanic Falls, Route 11 to Lewiston, Route 202 to Augusta, then up Route 9 through China Lake and Unity and _______ to Bangor." What fictional city is missing from Mrs. Todd's directions?

a. Derry
b. Castle Rock
c. Haven
d. 'Salem's Lot

122 What did they call the first water lift from the Martian ice-caps?

a. Arrowstone Project
b. Operation Straw
c. Project Bradbury
d. Project Aqua-1

123 Who invented the Jaunt process?

a. Edgar Carson
b. James Buffington
c. Rudy Foggia
d. Victor Carune

124 What year was Mike Scollay's sister's wedding?

a. 1936
b. 1927
c. 1930
d. 1938

125 What instrument does the narrator of "The Wedding Gig" play?

a. Saxophone
b. Trumpet
c. Cornet
d. Clarinet

126 What kind of word processor does Richard Hagstrom get as a gift?

a. Wang
b. IBM
c. Macintosh
d. Hybrid

127 Which short story is set at 249B East 35th?

a. "The Cat From Hell"
b. "The Wedding Gig"
c. "The Man Who Would Not Shake Hands"
d. "The Man Who Loved Flowers"

128 Which short story features a character named Henry Brower?

a. "The Man Who Would Not Shake Hands"
b. "The Monkey"
c. "Mrs. Todd's Shortcut"
d. "Here There Be Tygers"

129 Which short story features a character named Excellent Montoya?

a. "The Man Who Would Not Shake Hands"
b. "The Jaunt"
c. "Beachworld"
d. "The Cat from Hell"

130 How many of John Delvers' mirrors remain in existence?

a. One
b. Five
c. Two
d. None

AA This is a view behind the walls in which short story?

131 What false name does Nona use?

a. Cheryl Craig
b. Norma Blanchette
c. Ophelia Todd
d. Mara Corday

132 What happened to Richard Pinzetti?

a. Killed by Nona
b. Bought a mirror with the reaper's image
c. Stranded on a desert island
d. Crashed on a sandy planet

133 Who said, "Madness is a flexible bullet?"

a. The agent
b. The editor
c. The agent's wife
d. The young writer's wife

134 Which of the following was written by Reg Thorpe?

a. *Shadow Dance*
b. *Underworld Figures*
c. *Air Dance*
d. *It Takes Two*

135 According to his introductory essay in *Nightmares and Dreamscapes,* where does King think he'll end up being buried?

a. Père Lachaise cemetery in Paris
b. At sea
c. In a pauper's grave
d. Goose Wallow, Wyoming

136 Which is the oldest story in *Nightmares and Dreamscapes?*

a. "It Grows On You"
b. "The Ten O'Clock People"
c. "Dolan's Cadillac"
d. "My Pretty Pony"

137 Which Edgar Allan Poe story is the inspiration for "Dolan's Cadillac"?

a. "A Cask of Amontillado"
b. "The Tell-tale Heart"
c. "The Pit and the Pendulum"
d. "The Gold Bug"

138 How was Elizabeth Robinson killed?

a. She was caught in the crossfire at a shootout
b. She cheated Dolan out of drug money
c. She was cheating with Dolan and tried to call it off, so Dolan killed her
d. Dolan killed her because she was going to testify against him

139 What did Robinson buy himself for Christmas?

a. A shovel
b. A Cadillac
c. A Nautilus machine
d. A pocket watch

140 What was Howard Fornoy's occupation?

a. Freelance writer
b. Fireman
c. Policeman
d. Truck driver

141 Who has "an IQ immeasurable by any existing test?"

a. Howard Fornoy
b. Richard Fornoy
c. India Fornoy
d. Robert Fornoy

142 Where did Miss Sidley get her gun?

a. A pawn shop
b. From her brother
c. From her father
d. She bought it in a dark alley

143 What kind of shirt was the boy who lost his Popsy wearing?

a. Boston Red Sox
b. Boston Bruins
c. Pittsburgh Penguins
d. Montreal Canadiens

144 In what town near Castle Rock did Joe Newall make his fortune?

a. Derry
b. Bangor
c. Haven
d. Gates Falls

145 "It Grows On You" is reminiscent to what later King work?

a. *Rose Red*
b. *Storm of the Century*
c. *Kingdom Hospital*
d. "The Langoliers"

146 What is the title of Peter Rosewall's novel?

a. *Air Dance*
b. *Blaze*
c. *Blaze of Glory*
d. *Fast Cars*

147 What was Howard Mitla's profession?

a. CPA
b. Plumber
c. Lawyer
d. Interior decorator

148 What game show does Howard Mitla watch?

a. Family Feud
b. Who Wants to Be A Millionaire?
c. Wheel of Fortune
d. Jeopardy

149 John Tell is mixing an album for what group when he first notices the sneakers?

a. Rock Bottom Remainders
b. Grateful Dead
c. The Dead Beats
d. Better Than Ezra

150 What is Clive Banning's grandfather's name?

a. Richard
b. George
c. Gerald
d. David

151 During what age range is most time my-pretty-pony time?

a. 10-14
b. 10-29
c. 14-60
d. 19-50

152 What game show is on while Katie Weiderman talks to her sister Lois on the telephone?

a. Family Feud
b. Who Wants to Be A Millionaire?
c. Wheel of Fortune
d. Jeopardy

153 Which of the following is not one of the Weiderman children?

a. Polly
b. Connie
c. Jeff
d. Bill

154 What is William Weiderman's profession?

a. Author
b. CPA
c. Lawyer
d. Dentist

155 Who was Stephen King going to visit when he had the idea for "Crouch End"?

a. Ramsey Campbell
b. Clive Barker
c. Peter Straub
d. Richard Chizmar

156 Crouch End is near what major city?

a. New York
b. Boston
c. Manchester
d. London

157 What family lives in the house on Maple Street?

a. The Lansdales
b. The Bradburys
c. The Campbells
d. The Kings

158 What is the fifth quarter?

a. Part of a pie
b. Part of a treasure map
c. A twenty-five cent piece
d. A region of Paris

BB Who is driving this car?

159 "Umney's Last Case" opens with a quote from what crime writer?

a. Sir Arthur Conan Doyle
b. Dashiell Hammett
c. Robert B. Parker
d. Raymond Chandler

160 In what format was "Umney's Last Case" first published?

a. E-book
b. Penguin mini-book
c. Screenplay
d. In *Nightmares and Dreamscapes*

161 Who was Vernon Klein?

a. Umney's last client
b. The world's oldest elevator operator
c. The superintendent of Umney's apartment building
d. Peoria's chief of police

162 Who was Umney's last client?

a. Vernon Klein
b. Samuel D. Landry
c. Arlene "Candy" Cain
d. Gabriel Heatter

163 Who is Samuel Landry?

a. Peoria's chief of police
b. The superintendent of Umney's apartment building
c. Umney's creator
d. The world's oldest elevator operator

164 Which story does King think "feels a little bit like the Bradbury of the late forties and early fifties?"

a. "My Pretty Pony"
b. "Suffer the Little Children"
c. "Dolan's Cadillac"
d. "It Grows On You"

165 In what state does "That Feeling, You Can Only Say What It Is In French" take place?

a. Maine
b. Massachusetts
c. Florida
d. Colorado

166 Where did Carol O'Neill meet Bill Shelton?

a. On a flight to Florida
b. At a school dance
c. In a bar
d. On a blind date

167 In what hotel is room 1408?

a. The Dolphin
b. The Stanley
c. The Overlook
d. Park-Plaza Hyatt

168 What year did the hotel in "1408" open?

a. 1900
b. 1905
c. 1910
d. 1915

169 Which of the following is not a Mike Enslin book?

a. *Ten Nights in Ten Haunted Houses*
b. *Ten Nights in Ten Haunted Graveyards*
c. *Ten Nights in Ten Haunted Castles*
d. *Ten Nights in Ten Haunted Churches*

170 What newspaper did Mike Enslin write for?

a. *The New York Post*
b. *The Washington Post*
c. *The Village Voice*
d. *The New York Times*

171 In what room was Rufus Dearborn staying at the Dolphin Hotel?

a. 1409
b. 1410
c. 1419
d. 1414

172 What did Rufus Dearborn do for a living?

a. Sewing machine salesman
b. CEO
c. Stock broker
d. Opera singer

CHAPTER 5
THE BACHMAN BOOKS

1 Who was Richard Bachman's widow?

a. Claudia Inez Eschelman
b. Tabitha King
c. Naomi Bachman
d. Valkyrie Ezra Curtis

2 In what year did Richard Bachman die?

a. 1996
b. 1990
c. 1987
d. 1985

3 How did Richard Bachman die?

a. Cancer of the stomach
b. Brain cancer
c. Struck by a minivan
d. Cancer of the pseudonym

4 Who was responsible for outing Richard Bachman as Stephen King?

a. Steve Lightfoot
b. Steve Brown
c. Brian Smith
d. Charles Verrill

5 The life and times of Richard Bachman were the inspiration for what book?

a. *The Dark Half*
b. *Bag of Bones*
c. *Misery*
d. *On Writing*

6 Which of the following did Richard Bachman not write?

a. *Thinner*
b. *The Regulators*
c. *The Long Walk*
d. *Desperation*

7 Which of the following did Richard Bachman not write?

a. *Roadwork*
b. *The Long Walk*
c. *Apt Pupil*
d. *Rage*

8 Which of the following was originally supposed to be a Bachman book?

a. *The Dead Zone*
b. *Pet Sematary*
c. *Misery*
d. *Cujo*

9 What was King's first choice for his pen name?

a. Richard Bachman
b. Guy Pillsbury
c. George Stark
d. Mike Noonan

10 What medical condition does Richard Bachman share with Ralph Roberts?

a. Pneumonia
b. Insomnia
c. Irritable bowel syndrome
d. Agoraphobia

11 What was original title of the first Bachman book?

a. *Getting it On*
b. *Rage*
c. *Second Coming*
d. *Cancer*

12 According to the list in *Wolves of the Calla,* which Bachman book is connected to the Dark Tower series?

a. *Roadwork*
b. *Rage*
c. *The Running Man*
d. *The Regulators*

13 What was the working title for *Thinner?*

a. *Gypsy Dance*
b. *Gypsy Revenge*
c. *Diet from Hell*
d. *Gypsy Pie*

14 Where does Charlie Decker go to school?

a. Blackstone-Millville Regional
b. Placerville High School
c. Hampton High School
d. Castle Rock Regional

15 What is Charlie Decker's school locker combination?

a. 19-19-19
b. 05-30-61
c. 06-30-00
d. 00-03-30

16 Which character did Charlie Decker not kill?

a. John Vance
b. Ted Jones
c. Jean Underwood
d. None of the above

17 Who is the main character in *Roadwork?*

a. Richard Dawson
b. Richard Dawes
c. Bart Dawes
d. Bart Dawson

18 What is the name of the hitchhiker picked up by Barton Dawes?

a. Sharon
b. Perry
c. Oliver
d. Olivia

19 What was Barton Dawes' profession?

a. Assistant little league coach
b. Manager of the Blue Ribbon Laundry
c. Manager of Taco Bell
d. Construction Company Foreman

20 According to a rumor, who raped a woman in Topeka?

a. Ben Richards
b. Charlie Decker
c. Jimmy Laughlin
d. Johnny Marinville

21 Who is the black man with the sword?

a. Ben Richards
b. Charlie Decker
c. Jimmy Laughlin
d. Johnny Marinville

22 Whose picture was on the wall in Ben Richards' room at the YMCA?

a. Gandhi
b. Hitler
c. Jesus
d. Yoda

23 Who is the first person to die in *The Regulators?*

a. Cynthia Smith
b. Cary Ripton
c. Jim Reed
d. David Carver

CC This man is on a diet caused by what?

24 What street do the Regulators take over?

a. Poplar
b. Elm
c. Maple
d. Willow

25 What movie is mentioned in *The Regulators?*

a. *The Dead Zone*
b. *The Mangler*
c. *The Shining*
d. *Carrie*

26 What character in *The Regulators* shares his name with a famous film director?

a. Cary Ripton
b. David Carver
c. Peter Jackson
d. Johnny Marinville

27 Which of these is not a Power Wagon?

a. Rooty Toot
b. Tracker Arrow
c. Dream Catcher
d. Freedom

28 Richard Bachman's widow discovered the manuscript of which novel in their attic?

a. *Roadwork*
b. *The Long Walk*
c. *The Regulators*
d. *Rage*

29 What are embedded in the cover of the lettered edition of *The Regulators?*

a. Knives
b. Bullets
c. Hatchets
d. Arrows

30 Pie Carver liked to say the word that described Marielle Soderson rhymed with what?

a. The thing you hit with a hockey stick
b. How you kick a football
c. How you throw a baseball
d. Witch

31 What caliber of bullets are embedded in *The Regulators* lettered edition?

a. .45
b. .357
c. .22
d. 30-30

32 On what date does the Long Walk start each year?

a. May 1st
b. May 15th
c. June 1st
d. June 15th

33 How many teenage boys are accepted to take part in the Long Walk?

a. 25
b. 50
c. 100
d. 19

34 Who did Billy Halleck hit with his car while otherwise occupied?

a. Angelina Lemke
b. Leda Lemke
c. Taduz Lemke
d. Susanna Lemke

35 What was Ray Garraty's number?

a. 42
b. 19
c. 13
d. 47

36 What is Ray Garraty's middle name?

a. Pete
b. Arthur
c. Randall
d. Davis

37 Who is the first walker Ray meets?

a. Hank Olson
b. Peter McVries
c. Art Baker
d. James Baker

38 Who gets his ticket punched after he comes down with a charley horse?

a. Curley
b. Percy
c. Olsen
d. Garraty

39 What is Hint Thirteen?

a. Save your wind
b. Slow and easy does it
c. Conserve energy whenever possible
d. No interference with the other Walkers

40 Which Walker gets the first warning?

a. Stebbins
b. Olson
c. Zuck
d. McVries

41 According to Hint Three, what will give a Walker blisters the fastest?

a. Athletic socks
b. Walking too fast
c. Walking backwards
d. Sneakers

42 How many Walkers were left when they crossed into Massachusettes?

a. 5
b. 10
c. 7
d. 3

43 Which Walker is the Major's son?

a. Garraty
b. Stebbins
c. McVries
d. Baker

DD A van brings death in which novel?

44 In what Massachusetts town did the Long Walk end?

a. Arlington
b. Boston
c. Cambridge
d. Danvers

45 How long does it take for a Walker to walk off a warning?

a. 1/2 hour
b. 3 hours
c. 2 hours
d. 1 hour

46 Who won the Long Walk?

a. Garraty
b. Stebbins
c. McVries
d. Baker

47 King picked the name Richard Bachman while listening to Bachman Turner Overdrive. Who is Richard?

a. Richard Nixon
b. The first name of Donald Westlake's pseudonym
c. Richard Dean
d. Ben Richards

48 How are the chapters indicated in *Thinner?*

a. By Billy's weight
b. By the date
c. 1, 2, 3, 4 . . .
d. Each title is named

49 How big is Billy's waist at the beginning of *Thinner?*

a. 28 inches
b. 34 inches
c. 42 inches
d. 50 inches

50 Which of the following is not one of Billy's law partners?

a. Greely
b. Lemke
c. Penschley
d. Kinder

51 Which of these Bachman books has been filmed?

a. *Rage*
b. *The Regulators*
c. *The Long Walk*
d. *Thinner*

52 During what year does *Roadwork* begin?

a. 1970
b. 1971
c. 1972
d. 1973

53 When was the first Bachman book published?

a. 1977
b. 1979
c. 1981
d.1982

54 Co-Op City, which features prominently in the Dark Tower series, is also part of the setting for which book?

a. *The Regulators*
b. *The Running Man*
c. *Rage*
d. *Roadwork*

55 To whom is *The Regulators* dedicated?

a. Claudia y Inez Bachman
b. Sam Peckinpah
c. Stephen King
d. Roland Deschain

CHAPTER 6
THE DARK TOWER SERIES

1 Who first published "The Gunslinger"?

a. Donald M. Grant
b. *The Magazine of Fantasy and Science Fiction*
c. Doubleday
d. Viking

2 Approximately how many pages long is the entire Dark Tower series in hardcover?

a. 1500-2000
b. 2000-3000
c. 3000-4000
d. more than 5000

3 Other than the Dark Tower books themselves, how many of his books has Stephen King identified as being related to the series?

---

a. 10
b. 15
c. 13
d. 17

4 How many years passed between the publication of the first Dark Tower book and the last?

---

a. 22
b. 15
c. 24
d. 19

5 Who was singing on Stephen King's stereo when he typed the first line of "The Gunslinger"?

---

a. Johnny Winter
b. ZZ Top
c. Paul Simon
d. Dr. Hook

6 During what month did King begin writing "The Gunslinger"?

---

a. June
b. September
c. March
d. May

EE From what other weapon were Roland's guns made?

7 During what year did King begin writing "The Gunslinger"?

a. 1969
b. 1970
c. 1971
d. 1968

8 How many years did it take King to write *The Dark Tower: The Gunslinger?*

a. 7
b. 12
c. 10
d. 15

9 One of King's inspirations was a poem called "Childe Roland to the Dark Tower Came." Who wrote it?

a. Alexandra Spring
b. Seamus Heaney
c. Robert Browning
d. William Wordsworth

10 King's idea of multiple, parallel universes was inspired by what author?

a. L. Ron Hubbard
b. C. S. Lewis
c. Isaac Asimov
d. Clifford D. Simak

11 What is the name of Roland's teacher outside of the classroom?

a. Walter
b. Cort
c. Marten
d. Vannay

12 What was Hax's profession?

a. Teacher
b. Cook
c. Servant
d. Stableman

13 Who gave Roland and Cuthbert food after Cort told them they couldn't eat supper?

a. Hax
b. Gabriel
c. Stephen
d. Alain

14 Who is Roland's mother's lover?

a. Steven
b. Marten
c. Cort
d. Hax

15 What were Roland and Cuthbert eating when they overheard Hax plotting against the Affiliation?

a. Berry pies
b. Fried chicken
c. Sandwiches
d. Table scraps

16 How did Hax intend to kill the people of Taunton?

a. Burn them in their sleep
b. Poisoned meat
c. Poisoned water
d. Shoot them all down

17 Where is Roland headed when Marten calls him into his mother's room?

a. To Cort's house to ask for his test of manhood
b. To the roof to masturbate
c. To his father's quarters to tell of Hax's treason
d. To Cort's house for his daily lesson

18 What is Roland's mother's name?

a. Gabrielle
b. Aileen
c. Susan
d. Alice

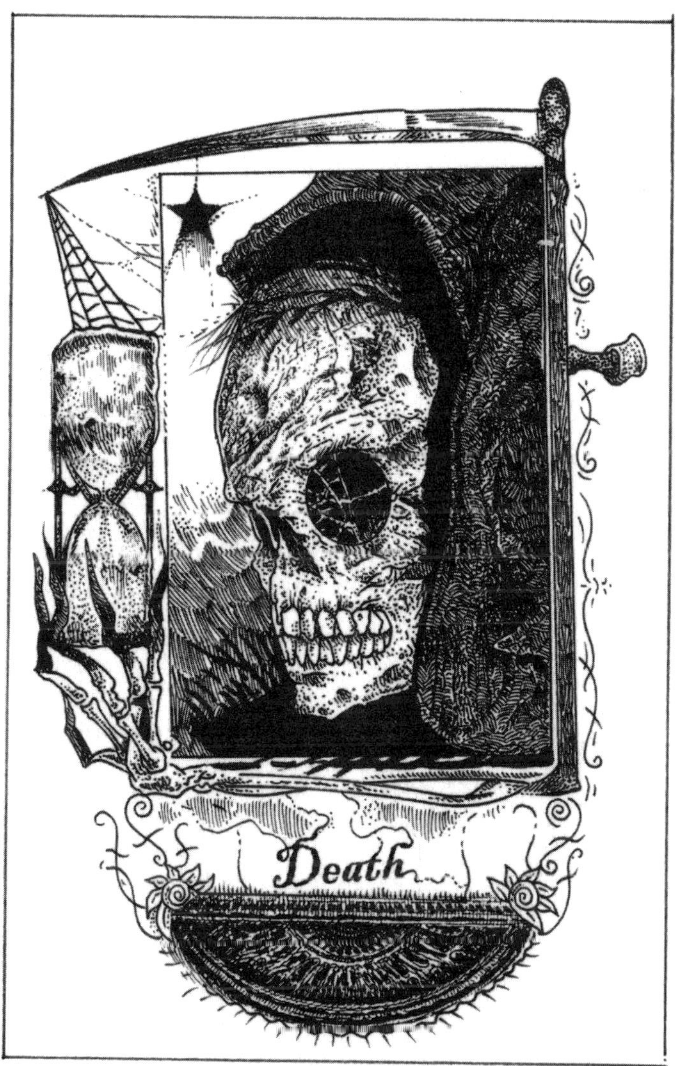

FF In Walter's seven-card Tarot reading, which card was this?

19 How is Hax punished for his crime?

a. Hanged
b. Shot
c. Beheaded
d. Poisoned

20 What does Roland put in his breast pocket for luck right before Hax is hanged?

a. A pinch of the bread sprinkled on the ground for the birds
b. A splinter of wood from the gallows' railing
c. The Chancellor of Keys from Cuthbert's deck of cards
d. A clover from the grass beneath the gallows

21 What type of birds flocked around Gallows Hill?

a. Rooks and ravens
b. Crows and sparrows
c. Robins and cardinals
d. Doves and pigeons

22 Where are Roland and Cuthbert told to leave bread after the execution?

a. On Hax's head
b. In Hax's pocket
c. Under Hax's shoes
d. In Hax's mouth

23 How old was Steven Deschain when he became a gunslinger?

a. 15
b. 16
c. 17
d. 18

24 Who must Roland defeat to win his guns?

a. Cort
b. Marten
c. Vannay
d. Steven

25 When Roland took his trial to become a gunslinger, how many years early did Cort claim him to be?

a. 2
b. 8
c. 3
d. 4

26 How many times did Cort tell Roland he would ask him to stand down and wait to take his test?

a. Once
b. Twice
c. Three times
d. Over and over again

27 How many times did Cort ask Roland to renege his gunslinger test?

a. Once
b. Twice
c. Three times
d. Over and over again

28 What weapon does Roland choose in his test to become a gunslinger?

a. Zoltan the raven
b. David the hawk
c. A spear
d. A sling

29 How old was Roland when he bested Cort and became a gunslinger?

a. 13
b. 14
c. 15
d. 16

30 If Cort had defeated Roland, where would he have been sent?

a. North
b. West
c. South
d. East

31 What is the name of Mayor Thorin's dog?

a. Kimba
b. Rigo
c. Sheemie
d. Wolf

32 What classic story did Susan tell Roland while in Hambry?

a. *The Little Engine that Could*
b. *The Wizard of Oz*
c. *Hamlet*
d. *Oedipus Rex*

33 What was Arthur Heath's good luck charm?

a. Rabbit's foot
b. German coin
c. Rook's skull
d. Two headed penny

34 The Pink Ball from Maerlyn's Rainbow is in Hambry. Where is the Orange ball thought to be?

a. Garlan
b. Lud
c. Dis
d. Verona

35 What was the name of the horse Roland took to Mejis?

a. Argento
b. Silver
c. Constance
d. Rusher

36 Who was the president of the Horseman's Association?

a. John Farson
b. Richard Stockworth
c. Herk Avery
d. Francis Lengyll

37 What is Rhea's last name?

a. Deloessian
b. Deschain
c. Dubativo
d. Coos

38 According to Rhea, who was Sheemie's father?

a. Eldred Jonas
b. Stanley Ruiz
c. Hart Thorin
d. Pat Delgado

GG What does this card represent?

39 What was Alain's father's name?

a. John Johns
b. Alain Johns, Sr.
c. Christopher Johns
d. Jasper Johns

40 Who sent Eldred Jonas west?

a. Fardo
b. Maerlin
c. Walter
d. Cort

41 How does Rhea replenish her energy?

a. She sleeps for eight years
b. She ascends to the third level of the Tower to be reborn
c. She feasts on a meal of blood
d. She gives her soul over to the Grapefruit

42 Whose mailbox marks the edge of Hambry?

a. Rhea's
b. Fran Lengyll's
c. Greta Shaw's
d. Mrs. Beech's

43 What did Brian Hookey wear around his neck?

a. A small bottle of graf
b. A horseshoe
c. An amulet with a picture of his mother in it
d. A reap-charm in the shape of a bell

44 Who delivers the knife that was intended to kill Steven Deschain?

a. Alain
b. Rhea of the Cöos
c. Farson's nephew
d. Hax

45 What's the last thing Cuthbert says before he dies?

a. No prisoners!
b. Hile!
c. Never surrender!
d. The Tower!

46 When Roland left Gilead in search of Walter, what direction did he go?

a. North
b. South
c. East
d. West

47 What was the ultimate downfall of the gunslingers?

a. Civil war
b. A surprise attack by Farson's army
c. Disease
d. Nuclear holocaust

48 Finish the title of this story: "The Little Sisters of _____".

a. Eliria
b. Eloria
c. Eluria
d. Elviris

49 Which "Sister" first brings drugged soup to Roland?

a. Coquina
b. Tamra
c. Louise
d. Michela

50 What is the name of the desert Roland crossed?

a. Sahara
b. Sasha
c. Mohaine
d. Garlan

HH What happened to this card?

51 What is the name of the bird Brown owns?

a. David
b. Zoltan
c. Midget
d. Gudrun

52 What kind of bird does Brown have?

a. Crow
b. Parrot
c. Blackbird
d. Raven

53 What did Brown try to teach Zoltan?

a. The 23rd Psalm
b. "I shoot not with my hand . . ."
c. The Lord's Prayer
d. The names of the guardians of the Beam

54 Who brings beans to Brown?

a. Cousin Mikey
b. Sister Mary
c. Pappa Doc
d. Roland Deschain

55 Where did Roland buy the mule that dies when he is staying with Brown?

a. Tull
b. River Crossing
c. Lud
d. Pricetown

56 What town did Roland tell Brown about?

a. Tull
b. Lud
c. Deschain
d. Gilead

57 What word does the man in black give to Allie so she can discover the secrets of death?

a. Ka
b. Chassit
c. Nineteen
d. Taheen

58 What mark did the people of Tull put on Nort's forehead?

a. A red eye
b. A cloven hoof
c. A rose
d. A pentacle

59 What is the major change in Allie's death in the revised *The Gunslinger?*

a. Roland spares her life.
b. She kills herself
c. Walter kills her
d. She begs Roland to kill her

60 Who owns the honky-tonk in Tull?

a. Allie
b. Sheb
c. Cuthbert
d. Cort

61 Who is Amy Feldon?

a. Cuthbert's girlfriend
b. A whore in Tull
c. A girl in Jake's class in school
d. A whore in Gilead

62 What song does Roland hear playing at Sheb's?

a. "Yesterday"
b. "Imagine"
c. "Hey Jude"
d. "Twist and Shout"

II What did Walter do with this card?

63 Where does Roland know Sheb from?

a. Gilead
b. Mejis
c. Pricetown
d. Lud

64 What is the best brand of whiskey served at Sheb's?

a. Bell
b. Star
c. Nickel
d. Berry

65 Who does the man in black bring back from the dead?

a. Nort
b. Allen
c. Sheb
d. Walter

66 Who is the crazy preacher living in Tull?

a. Sylvia Pittston
b. Sally Pritson
c. Susan Pondson
d. Sandy Pratt

67 What is Jake's last name?

a. Dean
b. Chambers
c. Sawyer
d. Holmes

68 Which of the following was one of Jake's father's bad habits?

a. Thcft
b. Uncontrolled anger
c. Violence
d. Drugs

69 According to Cort, what was made when the "Old Gods pissed over the desert?"

a. Devil grass
b. Sphagnum
c. Rhododendrum
d. Mescaline

70 What did Roland take with him from the way station?

a. A jawbone
b. A rib
c. A collarbone
d. A skull

71 Who in Roland's dream warned him that Jake was in trouble with the oracle?

a. Susan
b. Cort
c. Cuthbert
d. Walter

72 While Roland was talking to the oracle, what did he leave with Jake to protect him from it?

a. Flint and steel
b. Waterskin
c. His shirt
d. The jawbone

73 What adjective describes the mutants Jake and Roland encounter under the mountain?

a. Green
b. Four-eyed
c. Melted
d. Slow

74 What kind of meat does Roland cook for the man in black?

a. Rabbit
b. Lobster
c. Chicken
d. Salmon

75 During his Tarot reading, who does Walter say is depicted by the Sailor?

a. Roland
b. Walter
c. Eddie
d. Jake

76 What is sitting on the Prisoner's shoulder on the Tarot card?

a. Baboon
b. Gorilla
c. Chimpanzee
d. Orangutan

77 What tarot card represented Roland?

a. The Prisoner
b. The Sailor
c. The Hanged Man
d. The Tower

78 What is "the nexus of Time, the nexus of Size"?

a. The Universe
b. The Beams
c. The Dark Tower
d. The Rose

79 How many years did Roland age when he and Walter were done talking?

a. 2
b. 6
c. 8
d. 10

80 What is the name of the second Dark Tower book?

a. *The Waste Lands*
b. *The Drawing of the Three*
c. *The Gunslinger*
d. *Wizard and Glass*

81 What body of water does Roland reach after his palaver with Walter?

a. The Atlantic Ocean
b. The Western Sea
c. The Pacific Ocean
d. The Eastern Sea

82 What was the name Roland gave to one of the lobstrosities?

a. Larry
b. Lester
c. Lenny
d. Louis

JJ List the injuries this creature inflicted on Roland.

83 What is written on the first door Roland encounters on the beach?

---

a. The Prisoner
b. Death
c. The Sailor
d. The Pusher

84 From what year was Eddie drawn?

---

a. 1977
b. 1987
c. 1982
d. 1992

85 What is Eddie's addiction?

---

a. Heroin
b. PCP
c. Cocaine
d. Amphetamine

86 What is Eddie smuggling when Roland first meets him?

---

a. Heroin
b. Marijuana
c. Cocaine
d. Amphetamine

87 Who is Eddie trafficking for?

a. Fat Tony
b. Jack Andolini
c. Enrico Balazar
d. Tricks Postino

88 What is Eddie's brother's name?

a. Freddie
b. Mike
c. Henry
d. Steve

89 Where is Eddie heading when Roland first meets him?

a. Los Angeles
b. New York
c. San Francisco
d. Las Vegas

90 What was Eddie's seat assignment on the flight from the Bahamas?

a. 3A
b. 4A
c. 3B
d. 4B

91 Which crewmember of the "sky-carriage" was the first to be concerned by Eddie's behavior?

---

a. Captain McDonald
b. Susy Douglas
c. Jane Doming
d. Peter Thomas

92 What does the word "russle" mean to Roland?

---

a. To gather together
b. To stir up
c. To take a woman by force
d. To steal livestock

93 What was Eddie's last legal job in New York?

---

a. Garbage collector
b. Actor
c. Bartender
d. Pizza delivery

94 What answer does Henry Dean give to every Trivial Pursuit question?

---

a. Johnny Cash
b. Jim Morrison
c. Rolling Stones
d. The Beatles

KK Approximately how many days does it take Roland to travel from the first doorway to the third?

95 Who follows Eddie and Roland through the doorway to Roland's world?

a. Enrico Balazar
b. Tricks Postino
c. Jack Andolini
d. George Biondi

96 Who owns the "Leaning Tower" in New York?

a. Calvin Tower
b. Aaron Deepnau
c. Jack Andolini
d. Enrico Balazar

97 How many levels tall was the highest tower of cards Balazar ever built?

a. Three
b. Five
c. Nine
d. Twelve

98 Roland tells Eddie about two characters seen in another King book. Who are they?

a. Thomas and Ben from *The Eyes of the Dragon*
b. Dennis and Thomas from *The Eyes of the Dragon*
c. Stu and Fran from *The Stand*
d. Jack Sawyer and Wolf from *The Talisman*

99 Roland once saw Flagg change a man into what animal?

a. Rat
b. Dog
c. Horse
d. Bumbler

100 What is a popkin?

a. A sandwich
b. A soda
c. A donut
d. A beer

101 What is written on the second door Roland finds on the beach by the Western Sea?

a. The Prisoner
b. The Sailor
c. The Lady of Shadows
d. The Hanged Man

102 Where is Detta when Roland opens the second door?

a. At K-Mart
b. At Bloomingdale's
c. At Macy's
d. At Wal-Mart

103 From what year was Odetta drawn?

a. 1959
b. 1964
c. 1962
d. 1967

104 How old is Odetta when she is drawn through to Mid-World?

a. 21
b. 26
c. 29
d. 34

105 What movie does Eddie think about when he looks through the second door?

a. *The Shining*
b. *Carrie*
c. *Cujo*
d. *Misery*

106 During what year did Odetta lose her legs?

a. 1957
b. 1959
c. 1958
d. 1960

107 What weapon does Roland suggest would be ample protection for Odetta/Detta to use against the creatures of the night?

a. His guns
b. A sharp stick
c. A pile of stones
d. A dull blade

108 How many years separate Eddie and Odetta?

a. 9 months
b. 1 year
c. 3 years
d. 7 years

109 What was Odetta's father's profession?

a. Doctor
b. Dentist
c. Lawyer
d. Veterinarian

110 What fell on Odetta's head when she was a child?

a. A bucket of water
b. A brick
c. A piano
d. A flowerpot

111 What does Detta call her aunt?

a. Red Woman
b. Pink Woman
c. Green Woman
d. Blue Woman

112 Who is Jack Mort watching when Roland enters his mind?

a. Jake
b. Odetta
c. Jack
d. Detta

113 What was Jack Mort's real job?

a. C.P.A.
b. Stock broker
c. Garbage man
d. Bartender

114 What book does Roland see in Clement's Guns and Sporting Goods?

a. *The Gun Bible*
b. *Shooter's Bible*
c. *The Bullet Bible*
d. *The NRA Bible*

LL Who was the inspiration for this creature?

115 Who works at Clement's Guns and Sporting Goods?

a. Fat Tony Bianci
b. Clement
c. Fat Johnny Holden
d. Jack Mort

116 What was the site of the first penicillin robbery in history?

a. Doggin's Drug Store
b. Katz's Drug Store
c. Tower Pharmacy
d. Stark Drugs and Supplies

117 What is Roland looking for when he robs the drugstore?

a. Morphine
b. Aspirin
c. Keflex
d. Valium

118 What saves Mort's life when Andy Staunton shoots at him?

a. Bulletproof vest
b. A flask of whiskey
c. Staunton misses
d. A lighter

119 How does Jack Mort die?

a. Run over by a train
b. Shot
c. Run over by a bus
d. Burned to death

120 What was the title of the excerpt from *The Waste Lands* published in *The Magazine of Fantasy and Science Fiction*?

a. "The Bear"
b. "Bear and Bone"
c. "Door and Demon"
d. "The Demon"

121 Shardik the giant bear is named for a novel by what author?

a. Richard Bachman
b. Peter Straub
c. Richard Adams
d. Poppy Z. Brite

122 What did the Old People call Shardik?

a. Ursa
b. Mir
c. Maturin
d. Garp

123 What was growing out of Shardik's head?

a. TV antenna
b. Radar dish
c. Satellite
d. Mechanical bat

124 What beam is the ka-tet following?

a. Bear-Lion
b. Bear-Turtle
c. Bear-Bat
d. Bear-Fish

125 To Jake, who are Butch and Sundance?

a. ee cummings and Robert Browning
b. Robert Browning and Chaucer
c. Robert Browning and Dylan Thomas
d. TS Eliot and Robert Browning

126 What was on the last page of Jake's final essay?

a. Photo of a rose in a field
b. Photo of the Leaning Tower of Pisa colored black
c. Photo of an old fashioned train
d. Photo of a cowboy

MM Who fired the bullet that took Shardik down?

127 What are Calvin and Aaron doing when Jake first enters The Manhattan Restaurant of the Mind?

a. Arguing over the price of a Paul Sheldon novel
b. Playing backgammon
c. Setting up a book display
d. Playing chess

128 What year does Jake leave to join the ka-tet?

a. 1973
b. 1977
c. 1975
d. 1979

129 What is Jake's father's name?

a. John
b. William
c. Peter
d. Elmer

130 What is Jake's favorite sandwich?

a. Bologna and cheese
b. Ham and cheese
c. Peanut butter and jelly
d. BLT

131 Who drove Charlie the Choo-Choo?

a. Engineer Steve
b. Engineer Bob
c. Engineer Mike
d. Engineer Casey

132 Who is the author of *Charlie the Choo-Choo* in Jake's reality?

a. Beryl Evans
b. Richard Bachman
c. Calvin Tower
d. Betty Avery

133 What did the Speaking Ring look like to Susannah?

a. Stonehenge
b. A Roman amphitheater
c. Celtic burial site
d. Sutton Ho

134 What's the first thing Jake said when he returned to Mid-World?

a. You came! You really came!
b. You won't let me drop this time?
c. Roland! Roland, help me!
d. Where am I?

135 What is the name of the Billy Bumbler that Jake takes on as his pet?

a. Oui
b. Oy
c. Out
d. Oww

136 How did Oy get his name?

a. His family called him that
b. From the way he repeated the word 'boy'
c. It was on his collar
d. Eddie named him after his dog

137 What does the ka-tet find just before they reach Lud?

a. A car
b. A truck
c. A plane
d. A helicopter

138 Where were the remains of David Quick found?

a. The Cradle of Lud
b. Along a hillside in a sheet of flame
c. Beneath a deadfall of branches
d. In a WWII fighter plane

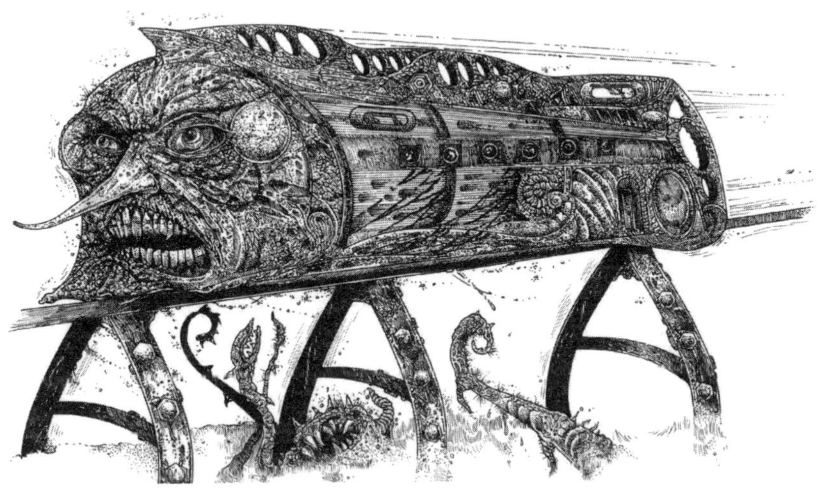

NN How does Blaine the Mono communicate with his central computers?

139 What symbol was on David Quick's plane?

a. A swastika
b. An American flag
c. A German flag
d. A red eye

140 What is the real name of Old Mother, who caught her newlywed husband hanging around Cassiopeia?

a. Old star
b. Lydia
c. Apon
d. Aunt Talitha

141 What are the names of the albino twins living in River Crossing?

a. Bill and Till
b. Ron and Jon
c. Si and Ti
d. Mercy and Percy

142 To whom did Roland attribute his combination of dry pragmatism and wild intuition?

a. Arthur Eld
b. Deidre the Mad
c. Steven Deschain
d. Cort

143 What is the name of the "Old Star" in Roland's world?

a. Vega
b. Caleb
c. Clotho
d. Apon

144 What was unusual about the people of Garlan?

a. They were black
b. There were oriental
c. They aged rapidly
d. The made immaculate Persian-like carpets

145 What is the name of the blind woman in River Crossing?

a. Abigail
b. Mercy
c. Talitha
d. Rita

146 Where is The Church of the Blood Everlasting located?

a. Dis
b. Calla Bryn Sturgis
c. Mejis
d. River Crossing

147 What is the last moon of Summer first of Fall called?

a. Demon Moon
b. Kissing Moon
c. Huntress Moon
d. Peddler's Moon

148 What is the gunslinger on top of the Cradle of Lud holding in his raised fists?

a. A dove and a revolver
b. A revolver and a crown
c. A revolver and an olive branch
d. A revolver and a fig branch

149 What color is Blaine the mono?

a. Pink
b. Green
c. Blue
d. Yellow

150 What does Blaine want?

a. Fairy tales
b. Theater
c. Music
d. Riddles

00 What does Tian Jaffords hope to grow in this field—and what is the field's name?

151 What is Blaine's termination point?

a. Topeka
b. Candleton
c. Rilea
d. Dasherville

152 Who was the last person to go near Blaine before Roland's ka-tet?

a. Ardis
b. Gasher
c. Scully
d. Patricia

153 How many destinations are between Lud and Topeka?

a. Four
b. Three
c. Five
d. Seven

154 Who collected riddles the way a lady collects fans?

a. Cort
b. Roland
c. Alain
d. Cuthbert

155 The UK limited edition of *Wizard and Glass* consisted of how many copies?

a. 250
b. 1000
c. 500
d. 2000

156 What color is the middle bar in the gate leading to the Emerald Palace?

a. Yellow
b. Black
c. Pink
d. Orange

157 What are Flagg's last words to the ka-tet?

a. "I'll get you my pretty..."
b. "Dare you, Gunslinger?"
c. "And have a great day!"
d. "Next time I won't leave."

158 What plastic figure sat atop the manuscript of *Wizard and Glass* while King was writing it?

a. Rocket J. Squirrel
b. Godzilla
c. Underdog
d. Mr. Peabody

159 In what book is the Crimson King first mentioned by name?

a. *Wizard and Glass*
b. *Skeleton Crew*
c. *Insomnia*
d. *Black House*

160 The Elegant Beef and Pork Restaurant is located where?

a. Topeka
b. Candleton
c. Lud
d. Lexington Avenue in New York

161 What was the unique automobile that the ka-tet came upon in Topeka?

a. Nozz-A-La Ghost
b. Takuro Spirit
c. Boing Boing Buggy
d. Honda Benz

162 To whom is *Wolves of The Calla* dedicated?

a. Tabitha King
b. Peter Straub
c. Frank Muller
d. Roland Deschain

163 How many full-page illustrations are included in *Wolves of the Calla?*

a. None
b. 12
c. 5
d. 19

164 What character from an early Stephen King novel lives in Calla Bryn Sturgis?

a. Father Callahan
b. Bobby Garfield
c. Rose Daniels
d. Charlie McGee

165 What does Walter call Callahan in *Wolves of the Calla?*

a. Shaman
b. Faddah
c. Mr. Poke
d. Donnie

166 Which Stephen King novel appears in *Wolves of the Calla?*

a. *'Salem's Lot*
c. *Carrie*
b. *The Shining*
d. *The Dead Zone*

167 Where and when did Father Callahan hit bottom and finally quit drinking?

a. Topeka, 1982
b. Queens, 1981
c. Topeka, 1979
d. Detroit, 1983

168 Where did Father Callahan visit the first time he went Todash?

a. Los Zapatos, Mexico
b. 'Salem's Lot
c. The Castle of the King
d. Topeka

169 What did Father Callahan witness on his first Todash trip?

a. Blaine the mono's crash
b. Jake and Roland leaving the Way Station
c. Ben Mears' funeral
d. Mia's transformation

170 Which writers were listed on the specials board when Jake and Eddie visit The Manhattan Restaurant of the Mind?

a. William Faulkner, Stephen King and Raymond Chandler
b. Raymond Chandler, John Steinbeck and Ben Mears
c. Stephen King, Anne Rice and Jeffrey Deaver
d. Anne Rice, Tom Clancy and John Grisham

PP She calls herself the daughter of none. What is her real name and what does it mean in High Speech?

171 Who said "Let God pick a winner"?

a. Roland of Gilead
b. Pere Callahan
c. Eddie Dean
d. Henchick of the Manni

172 How does Eddie impair Andy the robot?

a. Asks him for the password
b. Shoots out his eyes
c. Yells "19!"
d. Makes him divide by zero

173 The serial number of the Sneetch Eddie gives to Jake makes reference to what other work of fiction?

a. Spider-Man
b. Dr. Doom
c. Harry Potter
d. *'Salem's Lot*

174 Which of the following personas isn't Flagg in disguise?

a. John Farson
b. Walter O' Dim
c. Marten Broadcloak
d. Crimson King

175 To whom is *Song of Susannah* dedicated?

a. Frank Muller
b. Tabitha King
c. Robin Furth
d. Naomi King

176 How many stanzas make up *Song of Susannah?*

a. 13
b. 19
c. 21
d. 4

177 Which of the following is not of the Manni?

a. Henchick
b. Cantab
c. Maturin
d. Thonnie

178 Whose voice does Jake not hear in the Doorway Cave?

a. Greta Shaw
b. Benny Slightman
c. His mother
d. His father

179 What does Kra Kammen mean?

a. House of Bells
b. House of Voices
c. House of Travel
d. House of Ghosts

180 What business took over Chew Chew Mama's in 1994?

a. The Manhattan Restaurant of the Mind
b. Tom and Jerry's Artistic Deli
c. Dennis's Waffles and Pancakes
d. Tower Records

181 Which of these is not a partner at Trudy's law firm?

a. Guttenberg
b. Furth
c. Damascus
d. Patel

182 What kind of bag did Trudy use to carry her shoes?

a. Barnes and Noble
b. Borders
c. Books-a-Million
d. Betts Bookstore

QQ During what year did Eddie and Roland meet Stephen King?

183 Trudy Davenport compares her situation to that of Winona Ryder in *Girl, Interrupted.* What's wrong with this comparison?

a. *Girl, Interrupted* didn't premiere until December 1999
b. Trudy looks nothing like Winona Ryder
c. The character Winona Ryder played really was crazy
d. Winona Ryder wasn't in *Girl, Interrupted*

184 What is on the corner of First and Forty-sixth?

a. 2 Dag Hammarskjold Plaza
b. A pocket park with a turtle statue
c. A vacant lot
d. Park-Plaza Hotel

185 Who was the American president in Odetta's time?

a. John F. Kennedy
b. Lyndon Johnson
c. Richard Nixon
d. Gerald Ford

186 Which of these was not a control in Susannah's Dogan?

a. Emotional temp
b. Labor force
c. Body temp
d. Chap awake/asleep

187 Who is Mathiessen van Wyck?

a. Finnish Ambassador
b. Dutch Ambassador
c. Swedish Ambassador
d. Norwegian Ambassador

188 Mia named her "chap" after a character from what famous story?

a. *The Wizard of Oz*
b. *King Arthur*
c. *The Lord of the Rings*
d. *Alice Through the Looking Glass*

189 Where did Odetta Holmes go to university?

a. Columbia
b. Harvard
c. Brown
d. Morehouse

190 Where is the Dixie Pig located?

a. Sixty-first and Lexingworth
b. Sixty-first and Lexington
c. Forty-first and Second
d. Central Park West

191 What is the title of Stanza 7 in Song of Susannah?

a. The Castle Allure
b. A Game of Toss
c. The Ambush
d. Eddie Bites His Tongue

192 Who is "Old Double-Ugly"?

a. Jack Andolini
b. Enrico Balazar
c. Tricks Postino
d. John Cullum

193 Don Russert, who studies the walk-in phenomenon, is with what university?

a. Columbia
b. Harvard
c. Morehouse
d. Vanderbilt

194 Who is Sylvia Goldover?

a. Eddie Dean's old girlfriend
b. Henry Dean's old girlfriend
c. John Cullum's late wife
d. Calvin Tower's ex-wife

195 What baseball player's name does Eddie tell John Cullum to remember?

a. Tom Gordon
b. Pedro Martinez
c. Jason Varitek
d. Roger Clemens

196 How far is Bridgton from John Cullum's house?

a. 20-25 miles
b. Over 40 miles
c. 10-20 miles
d. Less than 10 miles

197 Where is the house Calvin Tower rented in Maine?

a. Dimity Road
b. Rocket Road
c. Turtleback Lane
d. Route 5

198 Which of the following is not part of the seven-town area around Stoneham?

a. Waterford
b. Lovell
c. Bridgton
d. Fryeburg

199 Where did John Cullum work after he got out of the Army?

a. Shawshank Prison
b. Maine State Prison
c. Chip McAvoy's store
d. Derry Jail

200 How much do Microsoft shares cost in 1982?

a. $10
b. $5
c. $15
d. $20

201 Whose death does Susannah not hear reported during her dream?

a. John Kennedy, Jr.
b. Martin Luther King, Jr.
c. Robert Kennedy
d. Richard Bachman

202 What Mississippi city did Odetta visit during her protest years?

a. Oxford
b. Jackson
c. Biloxi
d. Tupelo

RR What Robert Browning poem inspired the name of this creature?

203 What is the official name of the Fedic Dogan?

a. Arc 19 Experimental Station
b. Arc 16 Experimental Station
c. Arc 99 Experimental Station
d. Arc 13 Experimental Station

204 Mia was responsible for the death of Roy Depape's brother. What was his name?

a. Eldred
b. Ronald
c. Amos
d. Jonas

205 Who is Benzyck o' the Watch?

a. One of the Manni
b. A dead guard from Fedic
c. A NY city cop
d. John Cullum's friend in Vermont

206 Which of the following is not mentioned as being in the Bridgton shopping center?

a. Liquor store
b. Pharmacy
c. Supermarket
d. Laundry

207 Where in Bridgton does Stephen King live in 1977?

a. Turtleback Lane
b. Rocket Road
c. Dimity Road
d. Kansas Road

208 Who is Susannah's godfather?

a. Abraham Carver
b. George Washington Carver
c. Moses Carver
d. Noah Carver

209 What kind of vehicle does Stephen King drive in 1977?

a. Beamer
b. Jeep Cherokee
c. Mercedes
d. Porsche

210 Who was Zoltan?

a. A folk-singer and guitarist
b. A rock and roll singer
c. A hypnotist
d. King's college roommate

211 What uncle sent Stephen King to the barn as punishment for running away?

a. Otto
b. Roland
c. Oren
d. Jake

212 When Jake gets angry with the taxi driver who just missed Oy, who does he remind Callahan of?

a. Clint Eastwood in *The Good, the Bad and the Ugly*
b. Dustin Hoffman in *Midnight Cowboy*
c. Al Pacino in *The Godfather*
d. Dustin Hoffman in *The Graduate*

213 What does Stephen King "mail" to Jake?

a. A book
b. A key
c. A poem
d. The Orizas

214 How much money does Father Callahan steal from the hotel maid?

a. $39
b. $19
c. $119
d. $66

215 What is the maximum storage time at the lockers in the World Trade Center?

a. Twelve months
b. Twenty-four months
c. Thirty-six months
d. Forty-eight months

216 Why did Susannah and Mia get out of the taxi before they reached the Dixie Pig?

a. Susannah needed to think
b. Mia needed to stretch her legs
c. A bus was blocking traffic
d. They ran out of money

217 How much money did Susannah give to the busker?

a. $10
b. $20
c. $50
d. $100

218 Which of the following was not murdered in Mississippi in 1964?

a. Davis
b. Cheney
c. Goodman
d. Schwerner

219 What date is the first entry in King's journal?

a. July 12, 1977
b. June 6, 1977
c. June 19, 1977
d. July 19, 1977

220 How many letters did King's publisher get after *Pet Sematary* was released?

a. Five hundred
b. Three thousand
c. Nineteen
d. Ten thousand

221 The article in King's journal about walk-ins is written by a man who shares his last name with who?

a. Gordie LaChance
b. Thad Beaumont
c. Mike Noonan
d. Pops Merrill

222 How much time passes between NAL's first request to publish *The Gunslinger* and when King agrees to let them do so?

a. Three years
b. Six months
c. One year
d. Eighteen months

223 What do the locals call Route 93?

a. Rocket Road
b. Bog Road
c. Walk-in Road
d. Turtleback Road

224 What does "chussit" mean?

a. Fourteen
b. Sixteen
c. Eighteen
d. Seventeen

225 Who is the dan-tete?

a. John Cullum
b. Mordred Deschain
c. Irene Tassenbaum
d. The Crimson King

226 What kind of car do Eddie and Roland borrow?

a. Ford Pinto
b. Ford Galaxie
c. Plymouth Fury
d. BMW

227 When John Cullum was in New York on a 48-hour pass, which of these did he not do?

a. Visit Radio City Music Hall
b. Visit the Empire State Building
c. Visit the Statue of Liberty
d. Visit a prostitute

228 Where is Lamla, the taheen who follows Jake from the Dixie Pig, from?

a. Gilead
b. Lud
c. Algul Siento
d. Galee

229 Which of the following is not a robot?

a. Chumley
b. Stutterin' Bill
c. Andy
d. Nigel

230 What Stephen King book is Nigel currently reading?

a. *Carrie*
b. *'Salem's Lot*
c. *The Dead Zone*
d. *Firestarter*

SS What did Mordred's birthmark look like when he is in this form?

231 Which of the following King characters doesn't greet the ka-tet in Fedic?

a. Ted Brautigan
b. Danny Torrance
c. Sheemie Ruiz
d. Dinky Earnshaw

232 How old was Pimli Prentiss when he came to Blue Heaven?

a. Forty
b. Sixty
c. Thirty
d. Fifty

233 What did Paul Prentiss do in his former life?

a. Cop
b. Prison guard
c. School teacher
d. Worked for Enrico Balazar

234 Dinky and Finli o'Tego are both reading books by what author?

a. Peter Straub
b. Jack Ketchum
c. John Fowles
d. JK Rowling

235 How many Breaker dorms are there?

a. Three
b. Five
c. Seven
d. Nineteen

236 What direction are the freed Breakers sent during the battle of Algul Siento?

a. South
b. North
c. East
d. West

237 What direction does Irene Tassenbaum drive, according to the chapter title bearing her name?

a. North
b. South
c. East
d. West

238 What is "Chip" McAvoy's real first name?

a. William
b. Walter
c. Wallace
d. Wendell

239 What is Irene's husband's name?

a. David
b. Donald
c. Ronald
d. Reginald

240 During what month are Bridgton Old Home Days celebrated?

a. June
b. July
c. August
d. September

241 Which of these men was not a founding father of Tet Corporation

a. John Cullum
b. Calvin Tower
c. Moses Carver
d. Aaron Deepnau

242 What year did Aaron Deepnau die?

a. 1980
b. 1985
c. 1992
d. 1997

TT What are these creatures called?

243 Which Stephen King book did the Tet Corporation give to Roland?

a. *'Salem's Lot*
b. *Hearts in Atlantis*
c. *The Gunslinger*
d. *Insomnia*

244 What is Nancy Deepnau's middle name?

a. Rebecca
b. Odetta
c. Susannah
d. Irene

245 How much did the watch that the Tet Corporation gave to Roland cost?

a. $190
b. $1900
c. $19,000
d. $19

246 Which of these characters represents ego?

a. Feemalo
b. Rando Thoughtful
c. Fimalo
d. Fumalo

247 When did Joe Collins last visit the Dark Tower?

a. Six months ago
b. Two years ago
c. A year ago
d. Nineteen months ago

248 Which of the following stanzas in Browning's poem did King not circle?

a. I
b. II
c. XIII
d. XIX

1 The quote, "Sometimes being a bitch is all a women has to hold on to" comes from which movie?

a. *Dolores Claiborne*
b. *Rose Madder*
c. *Secret Window*
d. *Tommyknockers*

2 Who sings "I'm a little teapot, short and stout"?

a. Eleanor Druse
b. Ellen Rimbauer
c. Andre Linoge
d. Charlie McGee

3 As of this writing, which of the following novels has not been adapted into a movie?

a. *Carrie*
b. *Needful Things*
c. *Rose Madder*
d. *Cujo*

4 Who plays Charlie McGee?

a. Demi Moore
b. Kirtsen Dunst
c. Kate Hudson
d. Drew Barrymore

5 What poem does Harold Lauder read?

a. The Raven
b. The Dark Man
c. The Second Coming
d. The Waste Lands

6 What is the only movie directed by Stephen King?

a. *Maximum Overdrive*
b. *The Stand*
c. *Sleepwalkers*
d. *The Shining*

UU What kind of animal is pictured above?

7 On the cover of *Creepshow,* a movie poster for which film can be seen on the boy's wall?

a. *The Dead Zone*
b. *The Shining*
c. *Night of the Living Dead*
d. *'Salem's Lot*

8 Which short story was adapted for *Quicksilver Highway?*

a. "Rainy Season"
b. "Chattery Teeth"
c. "Dolan's Cadillac"
d. "Chinga"

9 What song did King want to have playing in *The Stand* that was ultimately replaced by "Don't Dream It's Over" by Crowded House?

a. Dirty Deeds Done Dirt Cheap (AC/DC)
b. Born in the USA (Bruce Springsteen)
c. Fun Fun Fun (Beach Boys)
d. It's the End of the World (R.E.M.)

10 Which film featured Alan King (no relation to Stephen)?

a. *Tommyknockers*
b. *Cat's Eye*
c. *Creepshow*
d. *The Mangler*

11 What was King's cameo in *Maximum Overdrive?*

a. Truck driver
b. Someone using an ATM
c. Bridge controller
d. A customer in the diner

12 Which adaptation has an ending only available on video?

a. *The Stand*
b. *The Shining*
c. *The Golden Years*
d. *The Storm of the Century*

13 Who said, "I hate Rock & Roll"?

a. Leigh Cabot
b. Larry Underwood
c. Richie Tozier
d. Glen Bateman

14 Which prominent King expert appears in the film version of *The Green Mile?*

a. Douglas E. Winter
b. Steve Spignesi
c. Tyson Blue
d. Michael Collings

15 Keith Szarabajka starred in which of the following?

a. *The Golden Years*
b. *Sleepwalkers*
c. *The Mangler*
d. *Children of the Corn 3*

16 David Morse appeared in all except which of the following movies?

a. *Hearts in Atlantis*
b. *The Green Mile*
c. *The Dark Half*
d. *The Langoliers*

17 What was Ellen Rimbauer's daughter's name?

a. Ellen
b. Rose
c. Eve
d. April

18 Which actor died during the filming of *Rose Red?*

a. Julian Sands
b. Kevin Tighe
c. David Dukes
d. Nancy Travis

19 Which personal favorite did King say was playing when the real terror started in 1951?

a. *The Day the Earth Stood Still*
b. *The Blob*
c. *Earth vs. The Flying Saucers*
d. *Invasion of the Body Snatchers*

20 Which of the following hasn't been in a Stephen King movie?

a. "Weird Al" Yankovic
b. Rob Lowe
c. Ed Harris
d. Max Von Sydow

21 What reappears regularly in *Creepshow?*

a. Ted Danson's head
b. A German shepherd
c. A marble ashtray with a figure attached
d. The boom microphone

22 How much was King reportedly paid for directing *Maximum Overdrive?*

a. $50,000
b. $100,000
c. $70,000
d. $250,000

23 The character played by Morgan Freeman in *Dreamcatcher* was renamed to what?

a. Curtis
b. Underhill
c. Johnston
d. Sarge

24 Harry Dean Stanton appears in which two Stephen King movies?

a. *The Green Mile* and *Christine*
b. *Storm of the Century* and *The Green Mile*
c. *The Green Mile* and *Dolores Claiborne*
d. *The Dark Half* and *The Green Mile*

25 Which band provided the soundtrack to *Maximum Overdrive?*

a. The Who
b. The Ramones
c. AC/DC
d. George Thorogood and the Destroyers

26 What was King's cameo in *Rose Red?*

a. Ghost in the garden
b. Pizza delivery guy
c. Reporter
d. Lawyer on TV

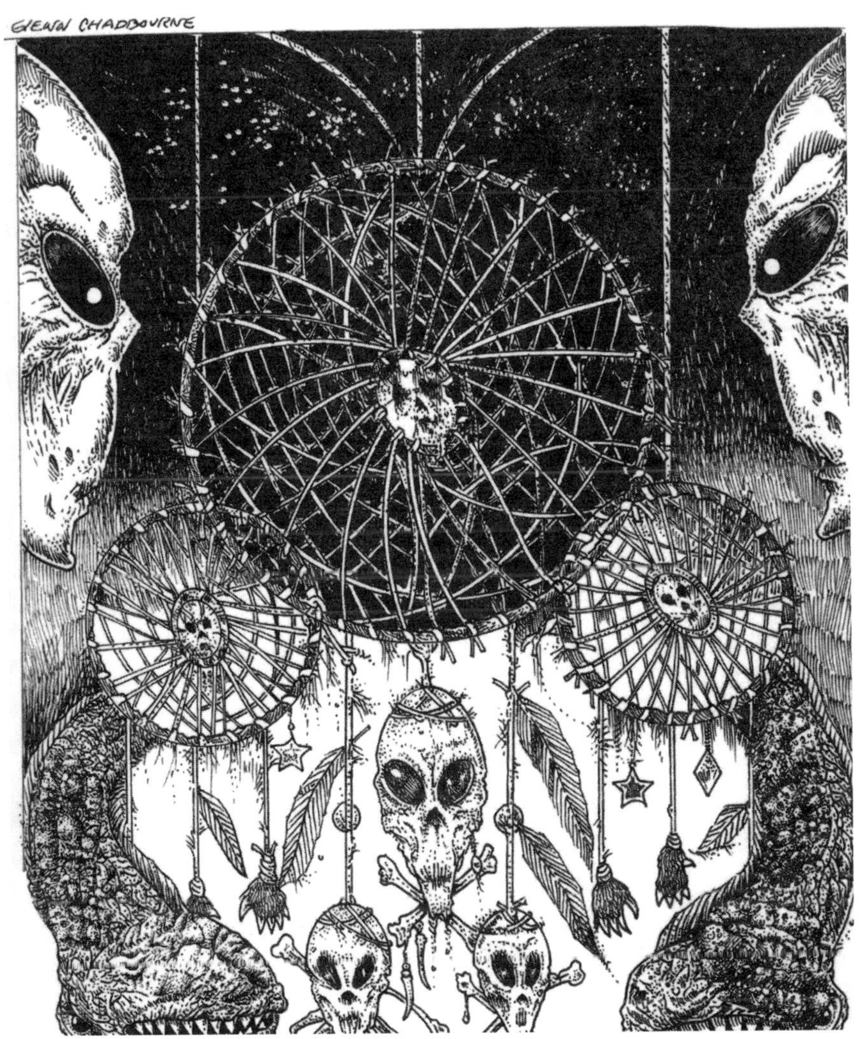

VV Who killed aliens in this movie?

27 As of this writing, how many Dollar Babies (the rights were purchased for $1) have been made?

a. less than 5
b. 5-10
c. 11-15
d. 16-20

28 Who played Gen. Starkey in *The Stand?*

a. Steven Weber
b. Stephen King
c. Ed Harris
d. Ken Olin

29 What movie did King sue (successfully) to have his name removed from the title?

a. *Dreamcatcher*
b. *Children of the Corn*
c. *The Lawnmower Man*
d. *Sometimes They Come Back*

30 What channel was Martha Clarendon watching when she met her unfortunate demise?

a. Cartoon Network
b. The Weather Channel
c. Comedy Central
d. Lifetime

31 What does Johnny Smith instruct his students to read on his last day at school?

a. *The Lord of the Flies*
b. *The Legend of Sleepy Hollow*
c. *Death of a Salesman*
d. *Romeo and Juliet*

32 Who played Frannie Goldsmith in *The Stand?*

a. Molly Ringwald
b. Justine Bateman
c. Ashley Judd
d. Heather Locklear

33 What actor, originally picked to play Jack in *The Shining* miniseries, starred in *The Storm of the Century?*

a. Timothy Hutton
b. Timothy Daly
c. Steven Webber
d. Tom Hanks

34 The father of which *Secret Windows* actor played Ellery Queen on television?

a. Len Cariou
b. Johnny Depp
c. Timothy Hutton
d. Charles S. Dutton

35 Colm Feore played a force of evil in which movie?

a. *Needful Things*
b. *Storm of the Century*
c. *The Mangler*
d. *Sleepwalkers*

36 Which movie adaptation was filmed in Maine at King's insistance?

a. *Stand By Me*
b. *Graveyard Shift*
c. *Pet Sematary*
d. *The Langoliers*

37 What is Cora Rusk's needful thing?

a. Elvis sunglasses
b. Elvis recordings
c. A bust of Elvis
d. Nothing

38 What type of machine crushed a kid in *Maximum Overdrive?*

a. Steamroller
b. Soda machine
c. Plane
d. Automobile

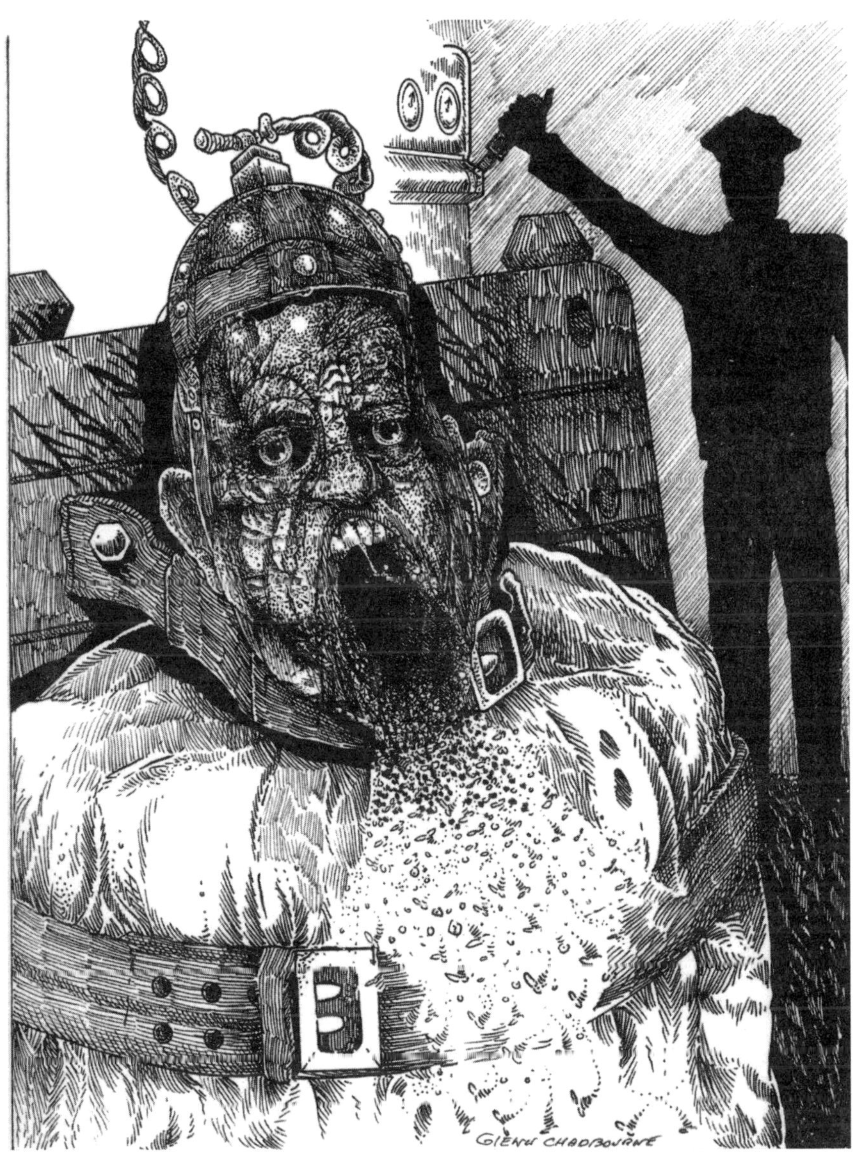

WW Who directed this movie?

39 What is the name of the university where the crate was found in *Creepshow?*

---

a. Harvard
b. University of Maine
c. Purdue
d. Horlicks

40 Stephen King wrote the production screenplay for which of the following?

---

a. *The Green Mile*
b. *The Stand*
c. *The Shawshank Redemption*
d. *Cujo*

41 What movie did Stephen King watch with the audience before speaking at the Jacob Burns Film Center in October 2003?

---

a. *Christine*
b. *Cujo*
c. *Carrie*
d. *Cat's Eye*

42 Who makes a cameo in the miniseries of *The Shining* as a ghost in the living room?

---

a. Peter Straub
b. Tabitha King
c. Frank Darabont
d. Stewart O'Nan

43 What short story was adapted as "The Lonesome Death of Jordy Verrill"?

a. "Weeds"
b. "The Crate"
c. "I Was a Teenage Graverobber"
d. "Harvey's Dream"

44 What actress has stared in the most King adaptations?

a. Kathy Bates
b. Molly Ringwald
c. Ruby Dee
d. Bonnie Bedelia

45 What was the last name of King's character in *Thinner?*

a. Haven
b. Castlerock
c. Derry
d. Banghor

46 What was King's character's profession in *Thinner?*

a. Pharmacist
b. Attorney
c. Teacher
d. M.D.

47 Who directed the short film "The Woman in the Room"?

a. Stanley Kubrick
b. George Romero
c. Frank Darabont
d. Mick Garris

48 Which of the following adaptations did King not have a cameo in?

a. *Quicksilver Highway*
b. *The Golden Years*
c. *Rose Red*
d. *Storm of the Century*

49 How many King-related TV-series has Craig R. Baxley directed?

a. 4
b. 0
c. 1
d. 6

50 What part did King play in *Creepshow?*

a. Jordy Verrill
b. Dexter Stanley
c. Harry Wentworth
d. Upson Pratt

51 What building was part of King's inspiration for *Rose Red?*

a. Marsten House
b. Winchester Mansion
c. The Sunlight Home
d. Thornewood Castle

52 What did Nadine Cross say just as the elevator door was closing?

a. We're all dead and this is hell.
b. Do you like my beautiful white hair?
c. Why are we here?
d. Do I look good in this dress?

53 Frances Sternhagen has appeared in which two King adaptations?

a. *The Stand* and *Needful Things*
b. *Misery* and *The Golden Years*
c. *Misery* and *Needful Things*
d. *The Golden Years* and *The Stand*

54 What part did King play in the *The Stand?*

a. Randall Flagg
b. Teddy Weizak
c. Bill Hapscomb
d. The Monster Shouter

55 Which actor won an Academy Award for a role in a King adaptation?

a. Tom Hanks
b. Kathy Bates
c. Jack Nicholson
d. Morgan Freeman

56 Which bit of movie dialogue, sometimes ridiculed by King, did he in fact write?

a. Outlander, we have your woman!
b. This ability to start fires may be just the tip of the iceberg.
c. They're all going to laugh at you!
d. A big man is pulling your ears off, Percy. I'd do what he says!

57 What does Polly Chalmers buy from Leland Gaunt?

a. An old baseball card
b. A high school jacket
c. A porcelain schoolboy
d. An azka

58 During what year did *Golden Years* debut?

a. 1989
b. 1990
c. 1991
d. 1992

XX Fred Gwynne stared as Jud Crandall in which movie?

59 What artist did Peter's paintings in *Kingdom Hospital?*

a. Bernie Wrightson
b. Michael Whelan
c. Ned Dameron
d. James Wyeth

60 Rob Lowe has played parts in which two King adaptations?

a. *The Stand* and *Needful Things*
b. '*Salem's Lot* and *Needful Things*
c. *Needful Things* and *The Shining*
d. *The Stand* and '*Salem's Lot*

61 What King adaptation made his friend Sam Raimi sick to his stomach?

a. *Maximum Overdrive*
b. *The Stand*
c. *The Mangler*
d. *Dreamcatcher*

62 What was King's cameo in *Pet Sematary?*

a. Trash collector
b. Minister
c. Bus driver
d. ICU doctor

63 What beverage, first seen in the Dark Tower series, also appears in *Kingdom Hospital?*

a. Commala-Cola
b. Nozz-A-La Cola
c. Redrum Rum
d. Flaggstaff Beer

64 What virus wipes out 99% of the world's population?

a. Captain Trips
b. The bubonic plague
c. The grateful dead
d. HIV

65 Who performs the song featured during the opening of *Christine?*

a. Ivy
b. Basement Jaxx
c. George Thorogood
d. The Rock Bottom Remainders

66 Of what clan was great aunt Bedelia the patriarch?

a. Torrance
b. McGee
c. Grantham
d. Verrill

67 "The Moving Finger" was adapted for which TV series?

a. *The Twilight Zone*
b. *Monsters*
c. *Tales from the Darkside*
d. *Quicksilver Highway*

68 Which of the following did Mick Garris not direct?

a. *The Woman in the Room*
b. *The Shining*
c. *The Stand*
d. *Riding the Bullet*

69 King's cameo character in *The Shining* is named for a character in which novel?

a. *Pet Sematary*
b. *The Shining*
c. *Cujo*
d. *Carrie*

70 Which *Kingdom Hospital* character thinks things are "ant-so-loot-ly delicious"?

a. The Emperor of Ice Cream
b. Blondi
c. Bullet
d. Antubis

71 What was the name of *The X-Files* episode written by King?

a. "Dingo"
b. "Dinga"
c. "Chinga"
d. "The Doll Who Ate His Mother"

72 What is the name of the mill that burned down on the site now occupied by *Kingdom Hospital?*

a. Courtland
b. Millwork
c. The Kingdom
d. Gates Falls

73 What was King's cameo in *The Golden Years?*

a. Doctor
b. Nurse
c. Hitchhiker
d. Bus driver

74 What causes an unexpected traffic disruption in *Maximum Overdrive?*

a. Drawbridge
b. Helicopter crash
c. Burned out traffic lights
d. Hydrofoil

75 During what year did the mill burn in *Kingdom Hospital?*

a. 1820
b. 1869
c. 1859
d. 1812

76 What did the mill in *Kingdom Hospital* produce?

a. Rubber
b. Uniforms
c. Plastic
d. Paper

77 Lewis Teague directed which two films?

a. *Children of the Corn* and *Firestarter*
b. *Needful Things* and *Tommyknockers*
c. *Cat's Eye* and *Cujo*
d. *Silver Bullet* and *Maximum Overdrive*

78 Which character from *Kingdom Hospital* shares his name with a town from the Dark Tower series?

a. Elmer Traff
b. Dr. Stegman
c. Earl Candleton
d. Eleanor Druse

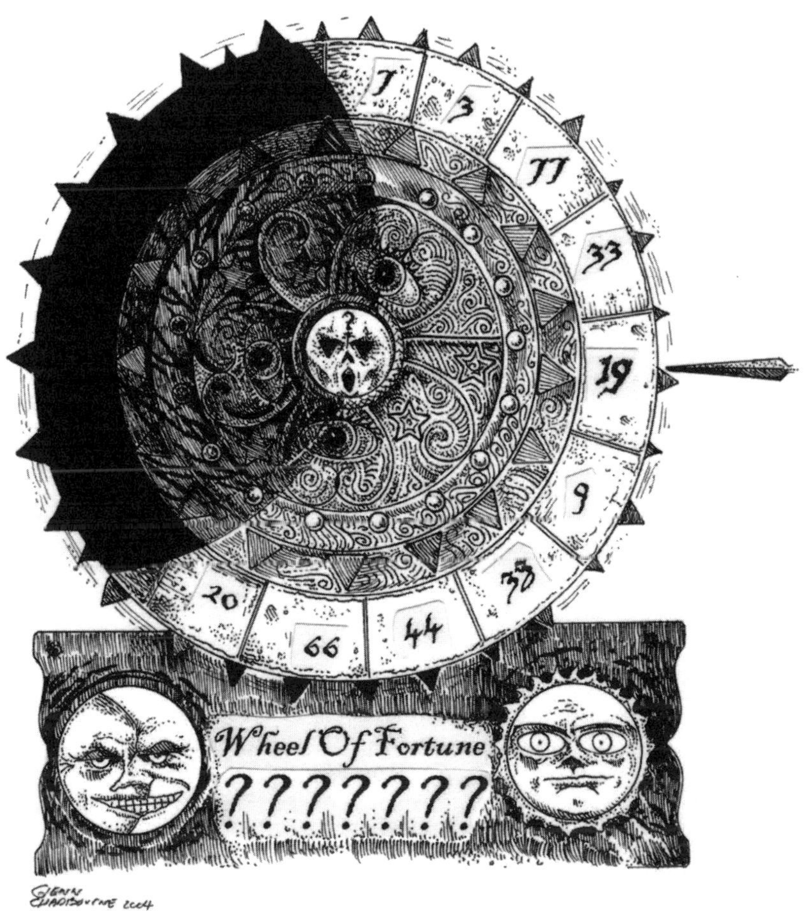

YY The Wheel of Fortune is the turning point in which movie?

79 What was the first King miniseries not based on one of his books?

a. *The Langoliers*
b. *Kingdom Hospital*
c. *Storm of the Century*
d. *The Golden Years*

80 What was King's cameo in *Sleepwalkers?*

a. Policeman
b. Cemetery caretaker
c. Coroner
d. Teacher

81 What object does King have in his mouth in his *Sleepwalkers* cameo?

a. Pencil
b. Lollipop
c. Toothpick
d. Straw

82 Which novel doesn't make a cameo appearance in *Kingdom Hospital?*

a. *Misery*
b. *Carrie*
c. *Bag of Bones*
d. *Rage*

83 What movie was the inspiration of the Anthrax song "Among the Living"?

a. *Misery*
b. *Apt Pupil*
c. *The Stand*
d. *Rose Red*

84 *Creepshow* pays homage to what 1950s horror comic?

a. *Tales from the Crypt*
b. *Archie & Jughead*
c. *Superman*
d. *The Fantastic Four*

85 Who has appeared in the most King adaptations?

a. Kathy Bates
b. Morgan Freeman
c. Ed Harris
d. Stephen King

86 What TV show featured a character named after and inspired by King?

a. *Tales from the Darkside*
b. *Tales from the Crypt*
c. *Quantum Leap*
d. *Incredible Stories*

87 Who did the cover for the *Creepshow* comic book?

a. Jack Kamen
b. Bernie Wrightson
c. George Romero
d. Richard Rubenstein

88 Who co-wrote the script for the Dollar Baby adaptation "Gotham Café"?

a. Bev Vincent
b. Brian Freeman
c. Rich Chizmar
d. Glenn Chadbourne

89 Which short story has spawned at least three Dollar Baby adaptations?

a. "Blind Willie"
b. "That Feeling, You Can Only Say What It Is In French"
c. "The Woman in the Room"
d. "All That You Love Will Be Carried Away"

90 Which actor from a King-based movie has gone on to direct several successful feature films?

a. Keith Gordon
b. Tom Hanks
c. Kathy Bates
d. Harry Dean Stanton

91 Which actor starred in both *The Green Mile* and *'Salems Lot* (2004)?

a. Tom Hanks
b. Rutger Hauer
c. James Cromwell
d. David Morse

92 Which King work has been adapted to the screen twice under different titles?

a. *The Green Mile*
b. *The Shining*
c. "Rita Hayworth and Shawshank Redemption"
d. "Trucks"

93 Which King film featured an actor who is also a knight?

a. *The Green Mile*
b. *The Shawshank Redemption*
c. *Hearts in Atlantis*
d. *Misery*

94 What do the film versions of *Misery, Hearts in Atlantis,* and *Dreamcatcher* have in common?

a. All were Castle Rock productions
b. All were written by William Goldman
c. All featured Kathy Bates
d. All were filmed in Canada

95 John Turturro appeared in which movie?

---

a. *The Mangler*
b. *Secret Window*
c. *Hearts in Atlantis*
d. *Dreamcatcher*

96 Which novel has been under option since before it was published, but has never been filmed?

---

a. *Black House*
b. *The Talisman*
c. *Rose Madder*
d. *Christine*

97 Which film did poorly at the box office but is frequently cited as a video rental phenomenon?

---

a. *The Shawshank Redemption*
b. *Dreamcatcher*
c. *Carrie*
d. *Hearts in Atlantis*

98 Which character in *Kingdom Hospital* is named after the creator of the Danish series on which it is based?

---

a. Eleanor Druse
b. Stegman
c. Carrie von Trier
d. Dr. Hook

99 How many cameo parts did King have in *Kingdom Hospital?*

a. 0
b. 1
c. 2
d. 3

100 Where was *Kingdom Hospital* filmed?

a. Mainc
b. Los Angeles
c. Vancouver
d. Florida

CHAPTER 8

NON-FICTION BOOKS, ESSAYS, REVIEWS, COLUMNS, AND LIVE APPEARANCES

1 Finish this quote: "Enter, Stranger, at your Riske:________"

a. For you are about to meet your Fate.
b. Here there be Tygers.
c. For all who enter, None return.
d. the Choice is Yours.

2 What is the name of the short story that won a contest and was printed in the paperback edition of *On Writing?*

a. "The Jumper"
b. "The Watcher"
c. "The Hitcher"
d. "The Runner"

3 What was the name of King's essay in *Mid-Life Confidential?*

a. "On Becoming a Brand Name"
b. "Bred Any and Good Rooks Lately"
c. "What Stephen King Does for Love"
d. "The Neighborhood of the Beast"

4 What was the name of King's column in *The Maine Campus?*

a. All the Trash
b. The Garbage Truck
c. The Garbage Can
d. The Campus Dump Site

5 King replaced what humorist on the back page of *Entertainment Weekly?*

a. Bill Thomas
b. Joel Stein
c. Sheila Moss
d. Larry Wilde

6 What did Stephen King publish in the 1999 MLB All-Star Program?

a. "Fenway and the Great White Whale"
b. "Brooklyn August"
c. "Head Down"
d. "Leaf Peepers"

77. Stephen King's signed books often go for over $100 on which online auction site?

7 To which fellow author did King dedicate *On Writing?*

---

a. Peter Straub
b. Tabitha King
c. Amy Tan
d. Stewart O'Nan

8 In February of 1987, on the advice of his literary agent, Kirby McCauley, King went cruising up and down New York City's 83rd Street. What was he looking for?

---

a. The bathroom
b. Prostitutes
c. Gargoyles
d. The Dark Tower

9 What recipe did King contribute to *The Riverdriver's Cookbook?*

---

a. Bonemash Bread
b. Grimy Ghoulash
c. Supper Slop
d. Lunchtime Gloop

10 King wrote the liner notes for a tribute CD for which punk rock band?

---

a. The Ramones
b. The Clash
c. The Sex Pistols
d. Green Day

11 What did King have next to his word processor while he wrote *Nightmares In The Sky?*

a. A bottle of beer
b. The heart of a small child
c. A ceramic gargoyle
d. A tiffany vase

12 In *On Writing* King says the road to hell is paved with what?

a. Run-on sentenccs
b. Oxymorons
c. Adverbs
d. Short sentences

13 In which magazine did "What Does Stephen King Do For Love?" appear?

a. *Redbook*
b. *Cavalier*
c. *Family Circle*
d. *Seventeen*

14 King wrote about the 2004 season of which baseball team?

a. New York Yankees
b. Boston Red Sox
c. Baltimore Orioles
d. The New England Robins

15 Who is King's *Faithful* co-author?

a. Jack Ketchum
b. Yogi Berra
c. Stewart O'Nan
d. Peter Straub

16 Why did King gaze up and say, "Not sure this is the best place for this reading!" during his *Bag of Bones* appearance in Seattle?

a. It looked like it was going to rain
b. It was held at the Overlook Hotel
c. It was held at a church
d. There was a crow flying overhead

17 What instrument does King play with the Rock Bottom Remainders?

a. Drums
b. Guitar
c. Keyboard
d. Trumpet

18 What is the name of the essay King wrote for the Bangor Historical Society?

a. "The Fire at the Black Spot"
b. "Bangor: A History of Horror"
c. "Black Magic and Music: A Novelist's Perspective on Bangor"
d. "Is Derry Really Bangor?"

19 Which musician has never performed with the Rock Bottom Remainders?

a. Nils Lofgren
b. John Cougar Mellancamp
c. Bruce Springsteen
d. Roger McGuinn

20 At what yearly gathering of mystery writers and fans did King speak in 1979?

a. Mystery Ink
b. Bouchercon
c. The Edgar Awards
d. Ides of Mohonk

21 King drove his Harley Davidson across the country to promote which novel?

a. *Needful Things*
b. *Desperation*
c. *The Regulators*
d. *Insomnia*

22 What was painted on the side of his Harley Davidson?

a. Skull
b. Vampire bat
c. Dreamcatcher
d. Spider web

23 After he arrived in California, how did King get his Harley back home?

a. The Hell's Angels president from Oakland, California drove it back
b. It was loaded into a moving truck and hauled back to Maine
c. King's bodyguard drove it back to Maine
d. King sold it to Jay Leno

24 What rock band consists of King and other authors?

a. The Tattered Remnants
b. All The King's Men
c. The Rock Bottom Remainders
d. Dirty Rotten Scoundrels

25 An animated version of King fought what other author on *Celebrity Deathmatch?*

a. John Grisham
b. Harold Bloom
c. Patricia Cornwell
d. JK Rowling

26 Where did King first meet David Duchovny?

a. During the filming of "Chinga"
b. At a science fiction convention
c. Backstage before a game show
d. At a restaurant

AAA Stephen King read three smoking-related stories on which audiobook?

27 What is King carrying in his American Express commercial?

a. A flaming taper and a sinister raven
b. A skull and crossbones
c. An American Express Card and a copy of *It*
d. A lit jack o'lantern

28 Which of these authors is a Rock Bottom Remainder?

a. John Grisham
b. Dave Barry
c. Clive Barker
d. Dean Koontz

29 The names of how many writers appear on the dedication page of *Danse Macabre?*

a. Ten
b. Five
c. Four
d. Six

30 Which of the following people appeared on *Celebrity Jeopardy* with King?

a. David Morse
b. Kathy Bates
c. Tom Hanks
d. Lynn Redgrave

31 The record company wasn't amused when King took liberties with the lyrics to which song?

a. Louie Louie
b. Teen Angel
c. Gloria
d. Stand By Me

32 On which three songs does King perform on the CD *Stranger Than Fiction?*

a. Bo Diddley / Stand By Me / You Can't Judge a Book by the Cover
b. Hit The Road Jack / Wild Thing / Proud Mary
c. The Boots Are Made for Walking / Johnny Get Angry / Rave On
d. Double Shot of My Babies Love / Chain Gang / Steam Roller Blues

33 Which of the following charities has benefited from a Rock Bottom Remainders performance?

a. The Wavedancer Foundation
b. Boston's Schools Libraries
c. New England Scores
d. Farm Aid

34 What book was released by the Book of the Month Club as a companion to *On Writing?*

a. *Secret Garden*
b. *Bare Bones*
c. *Secret Windows*
d. *Danse Macabre*

35 Who took the photographs that illustrate *Mid-Life Confidential?*

a. Amy Tan
b. Tabitha King
c. Dave Barry
d. Matt Groening

36 Why did Christina Starobin unsuccessfully sue Stephen King?

a. Simon & Schuster dropped her when King was signed on
b. She accused him of stealing her contract for the home he purchased in Florida
c. She said he stole her ideas for *Desperation*
d. She accused him of using her name in *Rose Madder* without her permission

37 What author received a two book publishing deal after King mentioned his book in his *Entertainment Weekly* column?

a. Richard Dooling
b. Andrew McCarthy
c. Mitch Albom
d. Ron McLarty

38 What book did Stephen King praise in his acceptance speech when he received the National Book Award?

a. *Drop City* by TC Boyle
b. *The Road to the Dark Tower* by Bev Vincent
c. *The Crossings* by Jack Ketchum
d. *Black Fire* by James Kidman

CHAPTER 9
MISCELLANEOUS

1 How many of King's books have been translated into Norwegian?

a. None
b. 1-11
c. 12-22
d. 23-33

2 The French translation of one of King's books is called *Danse Macabre*. What is the English title of this book?

a. *Skeleton Crew*
b. *Night Shift*
c. *Danse Macabre*
d. *'Salem's Lot*

3 The signatures for what limited edition were included on checks made out to characters and businesses from King's work?

a. *Prime Evil*
b. *Desperation*
c. *The Regulators*
d. *Six Stories*

4 Which of the following collections won a Bram Stoker Award?

a. *Four Past Midnight*
b. *Everything's Eventual*
c. *Nightmares and Dreamscapes*
d. *Hearts in Atlantis*

5 What kind of signed/limited musical instrument was made from a tree that appeared in a King adaptation?

a. Guitar
b. Harmonica
c. Banjo
d. Flute

6 The tree in question 5 appeared in what movie?

a. *Dreamcatcher*
b. *Stand By Me*
c. *Cujo*
d. *Christine*

7 Which character-story match is correct?

a. Todd Bowden / *Rage*
b. Peter Jackson / *Insomnia*
c. Melinda Moores / *The Green Mile*
d. Matt Babicki / *The Langoliers*

8 Which of the following stories was co-written with someone else?

a. "The Crate"
b. "Sladc"
c. "But Only Darkncss Loves Me"
d. "The Blue Air Compressor"

9 What is the title of the Dennis Downing album of instrumental music inspired by King's work?

a. The Dark Tower Music
b. Chanson de Roland
c. Suspense: Music Inspired By Stephen King
d. Thc Tcrritories

10 What artist had his name spelled wrong in the anthology *Legends?*

a. Erik Wilson
b. Michael Whelan
c. Thomas Canty
d. Ned Dameron

11 What is the name of the fictional tabloid newspaper that appears in several of King's stories?

a. The Insider
b. Inside View
c. Look Inside
d. Inside Lives

12 King did not sign which signed limited edition?

a. *Legends*
b. *999*
c. *Six Stories*
d. *The Best of Cemetery Dance*

13 Sheriff George Bannerman survived in which unpublished King work?

a. *Cujo Lives*
b. King's screenplay of *Cujo*
c. "Squad D"
d. "Stud City"

14 Which entry in the Celebrity Bear series represents Stephen King?

a. The blue #19 with a cross on its chest
b. The red #46 with a skull on its chest
c. The black #13 with "King of Horror" written on its chest
d. The orange #99 with "Everything Serves the Beam" on its chest

GLENN CHADBOURNE

BBB Stephen King and his guitar appear on the back of which of his hardcovers?

15 Actor Jeffrey DeMunn narrated which audio book?

a. *Dreamcatcher*
b. *Needful Things*
c. *The Girl Who Loved Tom Gordon*
d. *Riding the Bullet*

16 *Heroes for Hope* has a segment written by King starring which comic book heroes?

a. The X-Men
b. The Justice League
c. The Fantastic Four
d. SuperFriends

17 Estes Park Brewery brewed a special beer for the Stanley Hotel. What is printed on the door on the beer bottle label?

a. Insomnia
b. Cujo Ale
c. Carrie's Lot
d. Redrum ELA

18 Where was King when he said, "I'm warped and I like to scare people."?

a. On the *Tonight Show* with Jay Leno
c. On the road with the Rock Bottom Remainders
b. At the White House
d. Billerica (Mass. Public Library)

19 What does King describe as "like sitting on a suitcase"?

a. Dieting
b. Adapting his own novels to the screen
c. Exercising
d. Doing a second draft of a novel

20 Who did King say died of cancer of the pseudonym?

a. Stephen King
b. George Stark
c. Danielle Steele
d. Richard Bachman

21 In 1993, *Entertainment Weekly* named five films that King considers his favorites. Which of these wasn't on the list?

a. *Being There*
b. *Casablanca*
c. *The Wild Bunch*
d. *The Good, the Bad, and the Ugly*

22 To which American author is King compared in *The Columbia Encyclopedia?*

a. Dean Koontz
b. Bram Stoker
c. Edgar Allan Poe
d. Peter Straub

23 How many signed copies of the anthology *Legends* were produced?

a. 500
b. 250
c. 100
d. 50

24 In all of King's works, how many of the main characters are also writers?

a. 10
c. 25
b. 13
d. We don't know

25 What was the top King-related item auctioned off in support of the Bangor YMCA in early 1998?

a. Your name as a character in future book
b. Back stage passes to the Rock Bottom Remainders Concert in Bangor
c. Dinner with Stephen King
d. A complete set of Signed Limited books

26 Which sports team gave out Stephen King Bobble-head dolls in August 2004?

a. Bangor Mighty Ducks
b. Boston Red Sox
c. New York Yankees
d. Lowell Spinners

HINTS

CHAPTER 1: BIOGRAPHY

1) Maybe that's why they filmed *Stand By Me* in Oregon
2) Same as his father
3) Baby duck?
4) What rainbows do
5) That had to suck
6) The hawk
7) The year the Polaroid Land camera was invented
8) Don't read question 9 yet
9) Where the Saint Marys and Saint Joseph rivers join to form the Maumee River
10) A sad, sad story
11) A wascally character
12) She paid him a quarter
13) The Texas tower shooter
14) A magnificent number
15) A kind of cracker
16) His brother's creation
17) A school friend
18) Some of his high school stories recently turned up in *The Drum*
19) Some stories can't wait to be written—they just come out
20) In *Comics Review* in 1967

21) “The Glass Floor” in *Startling Mystery Stories*
22) aka Dorcas
23) Pinette in the distant past
24) The year *A Clockwork Orange* was released
25) In the library
26) Together with Ellery Queen, the three of them would be well on their way to a good game of chess
27) Those who can’t do something, do this, according to the old saying
28) His first-year salary was $6400
29) There’s an ongoing theme to these last few questions
30) She’s not doomed to repeat it
31) Girl-boy-boy
32) Delicate creature
33) Edited King’s first five books
34) It uses electricity
35) Good for quite a few of the above
36) Also the name of a character in *Carrie*
37) It’s that little dent under your nose
38) Ten years after they were married
39) It was inspiration for *Bag of Bones*
40) Not generally associated with writing
41) Are there really that many languages?
42) One of the answers is its unofficial name
43) Just before *Bag of Bones* was published
44) The name alludes to writing
45) He was originally going to be Guy Pillsbury
46) His personal assistant at the time
47) Some direction is necessary
48) A pivotal year in the Dark Tower series
49) Like many kids
50) Add up the digits
51) By Don Robertson
52) Over a half million copies served
53) There just aren’t enough hours in the day
54) Like “1408”
55) Fewer than the number of movies based on his books and stories
56) “The Breathing Method”

CHAPTER 2: NOVELS

1) Pure as the driven snow
2) She was a chambermaid
3) The nickname of an NHL goaltender
4) A novel of burning desire
5) A teen gang plans to start a race riot there
6) I tot I taw a puddy tat
7) The "affiliation brats" had a bunch of these
8) Who also had mother issues
9) The subject of *Faithful*
10) He didn't light any fires, though
11) Might make a great reality TV show
12) He came up with this one on his own
13) Replaced by David Palladino in the Viking edition
14) He helps out Thad Beaumont
15) He gets to meet a lot of famous people
16) She didn't have a ball at it
17) "promises to keep"
18) The same county that Bangor is in
19) Hi-o!
20) It became part of a family ritual
21) Because Jack cut him from the team
22) It must have been a *big* package
23) The rabbit, silly
24) My heart burns there too
25) Or the "hayocks" for short
26) The band leader's last name was Vreck
27) Their only King title
28) Killed by King Roland of Delain
29) Most of it, in other words
30) The word means an elephant trainer
31) Put a glass of water next to him and it was the water that looked vivacious
32) A regal name
33) I'd like to buy a vowel
34) King won a medal from them recently, too
35) Not of the vampire variety
36) A big man with scars on his face and a bald head
37) He bet $51
38) A drunk driver
39) It didn't land on its feet this time

40) Roland uses this name for a lobstrocity
41) When they said "west" they meant it
42) Home of the Villageburger Deluxe
43) It's the first Castle Rock story
44) Site of a famous battle in 1415
45) The name of a character in *The Stand*
46) Bill Fullerton, Second Selectman, wanted his job
47) Setting for "The Library Policeman"
48) Peter and Thomas' mother
49) Home to Stu Redman
50) Same as her creator
51) Not sure the town is still there
52) An allusion to his drinking problem?
53) He bought a pipe and promised to play a prank on Sally Ratcliffe
54) So he could rip that old motor out of Richie Simms's International
55) Norm called her "the slutty high-yellow gal"
56) He's barely a centenarian
57) A little bit of Van Gogh
58) The only good picture of the clock shows a quarter to ten, over five hours early
59) Not a very original name
60) Alludes to Peter's escape plan
61) Don't feed the piranhas
62) At least he wasn't pompous enough to put a capital letter in the middle
63) A steward at Sunlight Gardner's home
64) The book already has its own serial killer
65) Same kind his creator rode cross-country while promoting *Insomnia*
66) Hey, Abbbboottt
67) It's those twenty mile "hikes" that do it
68) Trees. Every page you turn, more trees
69) Not just four
70) Heard on Witcham Street
71) A gift from Jim Gardener in 1976
72) Father Callahan goes there on a todash journey for Ben's funeral
73) It ended up having a *lot* of houses in it
74) Wonder if she had her taxes done
75) Johnny Marinville wasn't driving
76) Maybe its name was Tony
77) Named for the son of Zeus and Europa and the brother of Minos, king of Crete
78) She was fifteen years old, myopic and played the record player loud
79) Raw, no less. Ewwww.

80) Christine didn't like the arches
81) King's wife made him change it
82) The only person Jessie told the complete truth to
83) His parents should have been shot
84) Sounds like a hair replacement drug
85) What all actors really want
86) His name means "he who bears Christ"
87) His parking tickets weren't winners
88) He lost his farmhouse as a result of his kindness
89) Now he's older and wiser
90) Halfway between Wichita and Dodge City as the crow flies
91) "I am a slow learner, but I am a fast driver"
92) Named after the dog
93) Begins with R. Boy, that helps, doesn't it?
94) It could probably open up again after Gaunt was done with the town
95) I guess you could say he was disarmed
96) Vol.5, No. 1-2, 1982
97) It comes from the way he says his own name
98) One dot at a time
99) Plenty of time to recover for Halloween
100) 75 mm
101) Maybe she got her picture on the cover
102) The poet
103) "I never t'row dese tings out, me"
104) The home of the good guys
105) Perhaps one of the creatures from todash space
106) The Red Sox have that effect on some people
107) It's a kind of lily. So is "calla." Interesting, no?
108) He was on fire at the time
109) Excuse our French, but that ain't no way to treat a lady
110) Seems like a lot of trouble to go to for a carcinogen
111) Sounds suspiciously like King's editor
112) They're not dolls, they're *action figures*
113) She has an easy time lighting her candles
114) With a prick
115) Named for the 14th-century fortress palace of the Moorish kings
116) She begins at home
117) An oxymoron, of sorts
118) He was a teacher
119) . . . all the way
120) A highly symbolic name, given the eclipse theme
121) One of King's former homes

122) It's a made up name
123) Maybe he pines for them
124) A Biblical name that translates to "Tabitha"
125) Gorg, by name
126) Because it's blue?
127) I don't think these even exist
128) It's a "gender neutral" name
129) Submitted by someone named Emil Brodsky
130) Dracula was the first
131) His middle name was Anthony
132) Say ahhhh
133) Long enough to miss an entire presidency
134) She brought a cake
135) Must be a Jimmy Buffet fan
136) Fortunately not due to one of the Beams breaking
137) One of the books is *Machine's Way*
138) Either that or the boxing promoter
139) But she really wants to direct
140) He got maced for his troubles
141) Based on a real incident—he was thrown over the bridge
142) Once would have been enough for me
143) One wonders how they'd speak once they got it together
144) He didn't look Spanish
145) If you can eat two, they're free. However . . .
146) She was once a member of the Friends of Life
147) John Coffey was the prime suspect
148) How did they get Pie out of that?
149) "And whatever walked there, walked alone."
150) He must have picked that out himself
151) Sandy Koufax
152) A product of Sharp cereals
153) She later married Andy McGee
154) The chess match held near Derry's airport
155) The woman who edited his Stark novels was Ellie Golden. Coincidence?
156) "Sugaree"
157) But *It* came in second
158) A bit nuts, but a writer all the same
159) We're not quite sure what he is, but he's unpublished as far as we know
160) The town most often associated with King
161) Eleven bucks worth of gas
162) It's the color they turned after they died
163) He saved another one

164) Wasn't he afraid it might catch fire?
165) Apropos for a fantasy novel
166) There wasn't much to say about it
167) She was from *Rose Madder*
168) Four times Trisha's age
169) Danny Pintauro played him in the film
170) Not a novel
171) He's the man
172) Ewwww. No clues for this one. Gross. La la la. We're not listening.
173) Hopefully not the Crimson variety
174) Bobby and Carol up a tree . . . well, a Ferris wheel, actually
175) Polly Chalmers had it, too
176) After her father
177) The lettered state was bound in asbestos
178) About enough for a tank of gas these days
179) Jessie has a score to settle, too
180) Johnny's girlfriend
181) Sounds a little like another Roland's last name
182) The movie version is different
183) Emil sent us this one, too
184) On the west side of town
185) It's a Plymouth Fury
186) There wasn't much left for another story
187) What a pile of B.S.
188) It's *not* a Plymouth Fury
189) Same as *Storm of the Century*
190) They say it's better than one
191) It's not a Ford Pinto or a Plymouth Fury
192) Longer than you think
193) Pleased to meet you
194) Beep, beep!
195) C'mon, take a guess
196) Once you start looking for it, it's everywhere
197) His initials are R. A. J.
198) Looking a little yellow, are we?
199) The original Paydays didn't have chocolate. Oops!
200) Gift, numbered, and . . . I'm forgetting one . . .
201) His color vocabulary isn't that big yet
202) Take a gamble on this one
203) Didn't Dean Koontz write one of those?
204) The 'a' is an 'e' five times in the book
205) Just starting school

206) Amen
207) He wasn't playing with a full deck
208) By the author of an unfinished novel called *The Dark Tower*
209) A duo, not a trio
210) Sloat hated him
211) His father-in-law
212) Chesterfield, if you prefer
213) Not what you'd expect in a little girl's room
214) Darn rock chips
215) Let the buyer beware
216) A good way into the book
217) Don't stop him—he's on a roll
218) It's out past the mall
219) On Rodeo Drive, no less
220) Those evergreens burn really well
221) Another mouse had that name originally, too
222) Those were big territories
223) Any answer could be right . . .
224) But the joke was on Paul
225) One won the National Book Award, the other was about Vietnam
226) You probably know this one
227) But he's hoping to become permanent
228) I wouldn't have touched it, either
229) Don't confuse him with Ray Brower
230) Operated by Polly Chalmers
231) *Air Dance* was his other book
232) His first book, in spite of its title
233) In the book not the movie—the answer to this one is in *Cujo*
234) The name doesn't *sound* French
235) aka *Napkins*
236) He originally diagnosed Carolyn's brain tumor as tension headaches
237) A colorblind person might think it was black
238) It belonged to Win Purinton
239) Garrett Thibodeau was the town constable
240) At the Black Spot in Derry
241) Vicky Tomlinson became Vicky McGee, Charlie's mother
242) Hal was Warden at Cold Mountain Prison
243) She was good with kids
244) Kenny's grandfather
245) To Jack, he was an officious prick
246) He was Johnny Marinville's handler
247) Barton Dawes worked there, too

248) The world's oldest chaperone
249) Not one of the survivors
250) He didn't want them taking control of his TV
251) They literally turned money into ammunition
252) Charles D. to be specific
253) He witnessed Ed Deepnau's accident near the airport
254) A Biblical name
255) In Baltimore
256) Well, maybe on the front cover
257) Jack doesn't realize how true it will be
258) "just like in that book *Carrie* . . . "
259) Didn't it see her coming?
260) He could call it *Misery's Hippopotomus*
261) His name contains the name of a character from *Christine*
262) They were going to learn the national anthem on the way
263) One of the spies sent to Las Vegas
264) But she brushes after every meal
265) His new girlfriend
266) In the heat of summer
267) "The Bird and the Album"
268) He worked in Los Angeles
269) He took the family to Ludlow, Maine
270) Also the name of a recent film
271) Somewhere in Iowa
272) He went back to Boulder instead
273) Her card was green. Does that help?
274) Thirty-five million dollars—those'll be happy kids
275) He was hit by a car, so he didn't become an un-dog
276) The actor who played his namesake was the "blood-drinking human carrot from Planet X" in *The Thing*
277) By John F. Kennedy
278) His boyfriend
279) Off to see the Warden and his wife
280) His first limited edition, so maybe he wasn't used to all the writing
281) A real person
282) Named after a famous writer
283) Took him about half a year
284) Dirty Fordi
285) Couldn't heal himself, though
286) Her college roommate
287) He didn't buy American
288) Which is worse: bolts or acne?

289) One of Carolyn's sayings
290) Maybe nicknamed Peppermint
291) He turns up later in a basement in *The Dark Tower*
292) You can buy anything you want; all it costs is your soul
293) Was his wife's name Maude? An older lady? Hello? Is this thing on?

CHAPTER 3: NOVELLAS

1) Like Huey, Louie and Dewie to Donald
2) Dussander's banker
3) Also did *Wolves of the Calla*
4) Sounds like a bunch of lions at the San Diego Zoo
5) Did you notice the numbers add up to 19?
6) Played by Richard Dreyfuss in the movie
7) He got a camera for his birthday
8) Maybe this was how King imagined Danny as a teenager
9) Marty shot off some fireworks anyway
10) Was her poster on Andy's wall?
11) Of the imitation German variety
12) Were the feet green?
13) The 'pus' sisters
14) Maybe referring to his creator?
15) The good Reverend Lowe
16) Flagman on the GS&WM Railroad
17) Everybody loves him
18) Humping around kegs of beer
19) A Castle Rock story
20) It's a Vulture
21) It's also very hungry
22) His last words were, "She waits."
23) Author of "Crowfoot Mile"
24) Not published in a collection of novellas
25) One of the Hardy boys
26) Maybe he got a tan doing it
27) I can think of one scene that probably got cut
28) A name he wears with pride
29) nee Collins
30) The book's author and the screenplay writer for *Hearts in Atlantis* have similar names
31) It's in Junction City, Iowa
32) Because that's what he buried

33) He had to lay low for a while
34) The story of a woman determined to have her baby
35) Because he wanted Red to have a grand time
36) Loth of bushes
37) Because it was just that kind of moment
38) Written by William Golding
39) An unusual name
40) Ring out the old
41) Part of his Low Car
42) "Stud City" and The "Revenge Of Lard Ass Hogan"
43) Twenty miles from Playa Azul
44) Star of *The Dark at the Top of the Stairs*
45) Not available at Dunkin' Donuts
46) The man who spoke it didn't look exactly real
47) A country/folk singer
48) Peter Straub's home state
49) A rainy month
50) It hung on everyone else's walls, though
51) It was originally supposed to be a calendar
52) At least the good ones don't
53) Doesn't sound like a suggestion
54) The town that canceled the fourth of July
55) He has a bit of an identity crisis
56) It's why he starts biking
57) Actually a Brian Freeman short story
58) *From the Borderlands*

CHAPTER 4: SHORT STORIES

1) An auspicious number
2) A famous Maine company
3) The last story in *Everything's Eventual.* No, we don't know why.
4) A fine Chevy product
5) Home to George Romero. Maybe Dennis Guilder went there
6) From *Creepshow*
7) Nevada's capital
8) Maybe he used the truck to haul timber
9) North from Portland
10) He was more interested in mastering the ground
11) If he survived, he might have done it again to avoid publicity
12) A first for King story collections

13) Published by Stephanie Spruce
14) Televised on *Tales from the Darkside*
15) Chilly time of year, especially in Pittsburgh
16) Where's Don Quixote when you need him?
17) Lyers never win
18) I can't Tell you any more than I already have
19) Never, never ask the editor about this book.
20) We mean it. Never.
21) Also featured in *Firestarter*
22) There's a good reason the publisher is listed
23) Published in a standalone edition by Knopf
24) Stuck it where it didn't belong
25) Setting for the film *Stand By Me*
26) A riff on "The Telltale Heart"
27) The scary guy from Baltimore
28) Of the frozen variety
29) Ads featured Bea Arthur and Betty White?
30) You have to go to the borderlands to find this one
31) You have to show your ID to buy this one
32) South American
33) Maybe he had spring fever?
34) Ba ba ba-da-da, ba ba ba
35) Captain Tripps
36) A childhood friend
37) The digits add up
38) Home of the Sox
39) Set in a lost and found?
40) Add up the digits . . . it's everywhere!
41) Like Eddie on *Frasier*
42) "Harvey's Dream" and "Rest Stop"
43) His son was scared of the boogeyman
44) Only a trip to the Folger Library will reveal this
45) Ray Bradbury territory
46) 4-sure
47) They weren't killed alphabetically
48) You'd have to be desperate to accept
49) Bite the bullet and guess
50) Rickeeeeee
51) About a cent a word
52) She could be Sylvia Pittston's twin
53) A fair charge
54) Only the best for your mother

55) A Hamlet-esque handle
56) Also the name of a character in *Carrie*
57) She has some rather strange dietary needs
58) They have a forum
59) He takes it north with him
60) Early work
61) But there's probably no one left to sue
62) Bestselling e-book
63) Where's he going to find that many heads to wear them?
64) A baker's dozen . . . and then some
65) Originally published in *The Magazine of Fantasy and Science Fiction*
66) Published as "The Raft"
67) In whom we trust?
68) Everyone always forgets Idaho
69) It goes ding at the end of the sentence. You do remember what typewriters are, don't you?
70) She just might be coping with the End of Everything better than anyone else on earth
71) Seven or eight times if you count all the sequels
72) "Weeds", *Creepshow*
73) A book you could read on your stationary bike
74) *People, Places & Things*
75) King directed the movie version
76) And we all know there's a lot of those
77) One of them is more of a prose poem than a short story
78) If a killer were after you, you'd say this, too
79) Home of a scary dog
80) He first appeared in *The Dead Zone*
81) What kind of a hint are you looking for here? It's a number greater than 10!
82) Sometimes I still hear it in my dreams . . . then I wake up screaming!
83) All have something to do with smoking
84) He wasn't quite dead yet
85) Exercise is good for you?
86) In *Yankee* magazine
87) People die in all of them . . . well maybe. That's up to you
88) Increase the iron in your diet
89) I call that motivation
90) Also the name of an old TV series
91) A shaggy dog story
92) Batteries not included
93) Sully's girlfriend

94) Also available as a standalone limited edition from Lord John Press
95) No small weapons for this guy
96) The answer is just a few questions up
97) Do you really need one?
98) If someone called me that, they might disappear . . . and their little dog, too
99) In Maine
100) Maybe it's just me, but that sounds a little lewd
101) Butt, butt, you don't need a clue
102) In McBain's books, his name is always prefaced with "Fat"
103) First published in *999*
104) It appeared in *The New Yorker*
105) "Graveyard Shift"
106) Named for an author noted for surprise endings
107) I'll wait here while you look it up . . .
108) Gates Falls
109) But no character has that name
110) The speed ironer got the best of her
111) A rarer setting than you might imagine for a King story
112) He is described as an infallible predator
113) Kids who fail his classes come back. Again and again.
114) He should have just gotten it cleaned
115) He starts out small
116) Filmed as one of the early Dollar Babies by Jim Cole
117) "Charles. You may go to the bathroom and urinate."
118) In a Ralston-Purina carton
119) His real name is Harry
120) Not a "Beamer"
121) Where Bobbi and Gard live
122) Sheesh . . . did a kid think that one up?
123) He had a reputation for being eccentric
124) That was when jazz was jazz, not noise
125) Has three valves, a medium-narrow conical bore, and a deep, funnel-shaped mouthpiece
126) Described as "odd mongrel"
127) Stevens is the butler
128) Related to Ray, perhaps?
129) He said the rosary in pidgin English before he died
130) Two of them are in America
131) Norman Blanchette is who she gives it to
132) Changed his name to Pine
133) A lot of them probably feel that way about their clients

134) "Even the movie was pretty good, although not as good as the book."
135) Behind Aunt Rhody's barn
136) Shades of *Rose Red*
137) For the love of God, Robinson!
138) Wrong place, wrong time
139) He had some heavy digging in his future
140) Ironic that he ended up barely literate and scrawling
141) Also known as the Messiah
142) Taken from a dead German shortly after the Battle of the Bulge
143) Mario Lemieux's team
144) A mill town seen again in *Kingdom Hospital*
145) One of its stars is now on *Two-and-a-half Men*
146) The cover showed three Marines, one with a bandage wrapped around his head, charging up a hill with their guns firing
147) One of New York's lesser known
148) Phrase your answer in the form of a question
149) They make The Butthole Surfers sound like The Beatles
150) He taught Clive the importance of having a pretty pony
151) But it gets less so starting in the forties
152) I'd like to buy a vowel
153) Dennis is the other son
154) *Spider Doom*, among others
155) A future collaborator
156) The Kings lived near that city for a while
157) The last name of a famous writer
158) Better than being a fifth wheel
159) Author of *The Little Sister*
160) Years before "Riding the Bullet"
161) Looked like a cross between the Philip Morris bellboy and a rhesus monkey
162) Another author
163) Author of *How Like a Fallen Angel*
164) "The fiendish Bradbury who reveled in killer babies, renegade undertakers, and tales only a Crypt-Keeper could love."
165) The Second-Honeymoon State
166) They met again at college three years later
167) On Sixty-first street, around the corner from Fifth Avenue
168) The year the Mexican Revolution started
169) He's going to be praying real soon, though
170) Not one of your higher paying jobs
171) A few doors down, probably on the same side of the hall
172) Of the Singer variety

CHAPTER 5: THE BACHMAN BOOKS

1) She added a 'y' to her name in Keystone Earth
2) Year of a major earthquake in Mexico City
3) You probably won't die of this
4) He worked in a bookstore
5) George Stark wasn't a very nice guy
6) A twinner
7) A novella
8) She loved company
9) All in the family
10) It'll keep you up all night
11) A repeated statement in the book
12) Mi him en tow!
13) You won't find this in the supermarket
14) The valedictorian finished in first placer academically
15) The end of June
16) Someone survives?
17) Look down a question or two . . .
18) Her last name might be deHavilland
19) Similar to a job King once held
20) But he's not laughing now
21) Ah-nold
22) Joda?
23) Pit foreman of the Rattlesnake operation in Desperation, Nevada
24) It's a popular tree
25) We say "based on" in the most general sense
26) Can you believe he got all eleven Oscars?
27) But wouldn't it be a cool name for one?
28) His first posthumous novel
29) Bang! Bang! Bang! Bang!
30) Think about it for a while . . . you'll get it
31) We're not messing around here
32) Mayday! Mayday!
33) It's a nice round number
34) Thus begins the Lemke diet program
35) King likes prime numbers
36) Former governor of California
37) Neither Paul nor Mary
38) Sorta sounds like charley horse a little. Okay, very little.
39) Ralph Nader would agree

40) #88
41) Just don't do it
42) They're magnificent
43) #88, again
44) Last name of the housekeeper in *Rebecca*
45) 3600 seconds
46) It's debatable if anyone won
47) George Stark is another tribute to the same source
48) Good thing he doesn't lose a pound a day
49) Not a bad number . . . for a bust measurement!
50) This person becomes a partner of a different sort
51) King has a cameo in it
52) During the oil crisis. The last one, that is.
53) A paperback original called *Rage*
54) Is it in the Bronx or Brooklyn?
55) King was going to do a movie called *The Shotgunners* with him

CHAPTER 6: THE DARK TOWER SERIES

1) We're talking about the first of the five stories that makes up *The Dark Tower: The Gunslinger*
2) Viking/Scribner hardcovers
3) Listed in bold at the front of the final three books
4) First book was published in 1982
5) Might have been when he was writing it, too
6) See hint 5
7) The year the movie *M*A*S*H* was released
8) A baker's dozen, minus one
9) King studied him in a college class of Romance poets
10) He's also mentioned in *Hearts in Atlantis*
11) He's in session
12) As in: Your goose is . . .
13) And look at the trouble it caused
14) One of his many, many names
15) Yum
16) Not so yummy
17) Maybe Marten didn't want him to go blind
18) Not such an angel, though
19) Afterward, would you say he was well . . . oh, never mind
20) Knock on wood
21) Both associated with castles

22) In the shade, presumably
23) Old enough to drive a Takuro Spirit
24) Order in the . . .
25) This is different in the original version
26) I'm not going to tell you twice!
27) Well, okay, maybe
28) Thrust like stones at Goliath
29) Barely a teenager
30) The direction all young men are summoned
31) Maybe he eats burgers without taking off the wrappers
32) You're gonna put your eyes out with that
33) Not so lucky for the bird
34) Ah, Discordia
35) What's your *hurry* to look for hints?
36) Sounds vaguely Welsh
37) A rather dubious sounding name
38) It's Sheemie's real name
39) A name from *Winnie the Pooh*
40) Cort's father
41) But she doesn't have fangs
42) A kind of tree
43) He made horseshoes but he didn't wear them
44) It runs in the family
45) An obsession, for sure
46) The last part of news
47) A kind of social illness
48) Collected in *Everything's Eventual*
49) Maybe she was the cook?
50) Analogous to the Mohave in our world
51) Sounds like a magician
52) Nevermore!
53) He certainly lives in the shadow of death, but that's not it
54) Like the dictator of Haiti
55) Perhaps the price was right
56) Named after a 1970s rock musician
57) Once you've heard it, you see it everywhere
58) Satan was here
59) Maybe he doesn't feel quite so guilty
60) Someone from Roland's past
61) These questions are somewhat chronological
62) Take a bad song, and make it better
63) As told in *Wizard and Glass*

64) Drink enough, you'll see these
65) The weedeater
66) Someone else Roland almost met in Mejis
67) Rooms
68) Maybe he and Eddie knew each other
69) Potent stuff
70) Maybe it's not done talking yet
71) Even though King hasn't really invented this character yet
72) Still talking
73) Like mummies
74) Easter treat
75) He drowns, but no one saves him
76) A kind of ape . . . does that qualify as a hint?
77) Perhaps referring to his experience with Hax
78) What it's all about
79) Half a score
80) It has a number in it, but it's not "two"
81) It's where failed gunslingers are sent
82) After a Maritime Canadian folk song
83) Number six! Number six!
84) The stock market crashed on Black Monday that year
85) They don't come much worse than this
86) Great song by Eric Clapton
87) Call me Rico
88) Name of many Kings of England
89) The Big Apple
90) Seems like a picky question, but it's mentioned a dozen times
91) Maybe she had black eyes
92) Our word for it also begins with "r"
93) Dealing another kind of drug
94) The man in black
95) The lieutenant
96) He likes to build towers of cards
97) Pretty impressive
98) Still chasing the flagg
99) Of the howling variety
100) Tooter fish! My favorite
101) The two-faced Janus lurks behind it
102) Getting ready for the parade?
103) The year the Civil Rights Act passed
104) Old enough to rent a car
105) Reminds him of a Steadicam shot

106) Fidel Castro came to power
107) Better than a poke in the eye with a pointed stick
108) This is only stated once, and is seemingly contradicted elsewhere
109) Same as Richie Tozier's father
110) But not a ton of them
111) Maybe she was c-c-c-c-old
112) He's not dead yet
113) A bean counter
114) Maybe it belonged to the guy from *Secret Window, Secret Garden*
115) I'm guessing he's overweight
116) Look down
117) Roland calls it Cheeflet
118) Maybe smoking isn't that bad for you after all
119) Poetic justice
120) Shardik
121) Author of *Watership Down*
122) Russian for 'peace'
123) Just like on MTV
124) Shardik to Maturin
125) From his essay
126) Did someone here order pizza?
127) Bxe4!
128) The year *Star Wars* came out, but Jake didn't see it
129) Like the glue
130) Baloney
131) You'll have the answer and he's your uncle
132) Claudia wrote it in another reality
133) The only thing missing was naked druids
134) I've fallen and I can't get up
135) Sounds like he was named by an Aussie
136) If Oy had been female, her name might be Earl
137) Where's Tattoo when you need him?
138) Sucked through the Bermuda Triangle?
139) Not a very popular symbol these days
140) Part of the ancient realm now known as Turkey. Are these hints helping?
141) Tilliam?
142) His grandmother. I wish I had relatives with cool names like that
143) Lydia's husband
144) Seeing Susannah prompted the comment
145) The title of an excellent book by David Lindsey
146) Aunt Talitha showed it to them
147) We call it the Harvest Moon. Some hunt; some gather.

148) Look at the eagle on the back of a dollar bill
149) Patricia was blue
150) Picture a skinny guy in a lime green suit with question marks all over
151) We *are* in Kansas, Toto
152) Slain with blue fire when he couldn't answer a question. Hope you fare better. No pressure!
153) You have to look at the map for this one
154) One of the Affiliation brats
155) The number of miles race drivers go in Indianapolis
156) Technically, is it a color?
157) A smiley face
158) Bullwinkle!
159) Sleep on this one for a while
160) Along Blaine's path
161) Rando Thoughtful worked on their advertising campaign
162) He hears the voices in King's head
163) Go count them!
164) Last seen on a bus to New York
165) Here we are in Camp Grenada
166) The story of Father Callahan
167) Blaine didn't do so good here, either
168) All God's Chillun got Shoes
169) Proof he wasn't of the undead
170) Metafiction. Oops, we're not supposed to say that.
171) Not a man of god, exactly
172) Susannah does the same thing to another robot later
173) Serial # 465-11-AA HPJKR
174) This is who Flagg reports to
175) She knew when it was done
176) An auspicious number…just not the one you might think
177) The other one's a turtle
178) She was nice to him
179) I don't see this becoming a franchise
180) Not IHOP?
181) She wishes
182) It's a bookstore
183) Not in this reality, at least
184) ANOTHER GREAT SOMBRA/NORTH CENTRAL PROJECT!!
185) Why we're in Vietnam
186) She wasn't suffering hot flashes
187) Even though his name doesn't seem to match his nationality
188) Son of Morgana or Morgaine

189) In New York
190) Where Susannah-mio parked her rig
191) Roland and Eddie's first appearance in *Song of Susannah*
192) He was once fed to the lobstrosities
193) In Tennessee
194) Skank El Supremo
195) The Rocket, now plays for Houston Astros
196) Half an hour's drive
197) I have no idea where the name came from...it's a long way from Cape Canaveral
198) Where Stephen King lives
199) It's located in Warren, Maine
200) Worth over twice as much when Eddie leaves New York
201) Not him, but his alter ego
202) John Grisham's hometown
203) A surprisingly inauspicious number
204) A Biblical name
205) He and Rev. Harrigan have an understanding
206) King must get his beer at the supermarket
207) There's a street with this name in Derry
208) A Biblical name...there we go again!
209) With a nifty Indian stripe running up the side
210) Someone King knew at UMO
211) Not a very common name
212) Ratso Rizzo
213) Jake also found one of these in the vacant lot
214) Enough for two shares of Microsoft in 1982...with change
215) About nine months longer than they really needed
216) Ka might have put it there
217) He made her take it back
218) The voter registration boys
219) The 19s don't start until later
220) Not as many as there were copies of *The Gunslinger,* but almost
221) The Emporium Galorium
222) They first asked him in 1984
223) Presumably it's not very well paved
224) "Chassit" is nineteen
225) It means "little savior"
226) Apropos, since they're out to save the universe
227) He should have visited this lady instead of that other one
228) Sounds Biblical
229) Susannah calls a robot by this name, though

230) He operates on GMS, which reminds him on one of the book's characters
231) Maybe he's busy running a hotel somewhere
232) A little younger than Stephen King
233) Attica, to be specific
234) One of them is *The Magus*
235) They form a semicircle around the Study
236) Down, on most maps
237) Coincidence?
238) A Holmes has the same name . . . coincidence?
239) The name of Roland's hawk. Say it with me: coincidence?
240) At the very end of the month
241) Tet didn't sell books
242) John Cullum went first, in 1989
243) Its white over red cover is highly significant
244) Inspiration for *Bag of Bones*
245) I could buy a car for that amount
246) Goodmouth
247) What does time mean, anyway. Besides, he was probably lying
248) It begins, "A sudden little river crossed my path"

CHAPTER 7: MOVIES, MINISERIES, AND OTHER ADAPTATIONS

1) Movie and character have the same name
2) *Storm of the Century*
3) Optioned by HBO but unproduced
4) *Firestarter, ET, Charlie's Angels*
5) By Stephen King
6) Based on the story "Trucks"
7) All work and no play
8) First published in *Cemetery Dance* magazine
9) Daddy took their T-bird away
10) A trilogy of terror
11) "Honey? This machine just called me an asshole!"
12) Frances Sternhagen was one of the stars
13) George Thorogood, specifically
14) He contributed this question
15) A TV series – I'd like to buy a vowel, please
16) Adult Bobby, Brutus and the pilot
17) *Rose Red,* but that was the name of the house

18) The professor
19) The Sputnik launch, as told in *Danse Macabre*
20) It would be weird if he had
21) Used as a murder weapon (once), a soap dish (once) and an ashtray (four times)
22) More than for a short story—but not much
23) Originally named after a character in *Heart of Darkness*
24) One of them features a character named Harry Dean, but he doesn't play him
25) Who Made Who?
26) "Do this often? Hey, this is some place, huh? Is it haunted?"
27) More than a dozen
28) Star of *Needful Things*
29) There was no virtual reality in this 1970s short story, just some grass
30) She clearly wasn't paying attention
31) And then he went to sleep for nearly five years
32) She didn't wear pink
33) They seemed determined to hire *someone* from *Wings*
34) Star of *The Dark Half*
35) Canadian Feore played Glenn Gould and Pierre Trudeau
36) One of its costars was from *Star Trek: The Next Generation*
37) You can't see any blue suede shoes
38) Squished him like a bug
39) Also featured in "The Raft"
40) He wrote one for *Cujo*, but it wasn't produced
41) Dee Wallace Stone deserved an Oscar, according to King
42) Author of *Walpuski's Typewriter*
43) King starred in the adaptation
44) She was in *The Stand*
45) A clever pun
46) His place of business was the center of activity for the hit and run accident
47) He went on to direct two other King-based projects (as of this writing)
48) A made-for-TV adaptation
49) Two of them were related to *Rose Red*
50) Named after his editor
51) A shotgun house?
52) Commonly said of Las Vegas after a bad run of luck at the tables
53) One for TV and one for the big screen
54) He picked up Nadine
55) She didn't make any fried green tomatoes
56) From the original screenplay of *Children of the Corn*

57) To ward off her pain
58) The same year *Silence of the Lambs* came out
59) He's from Maine
60) Both made for TV
61) The steamroller got to him
62) The man in black
63) The un-un-un-cola
64) Also known as the superflu
65) B-b-b-b-b-b-b
66) From "Father's Day"
67) Not "Inc."
68) He's never done it for a dollar
69) Also mentioned in *Insomnia*
70) Named for an Egyptian god
71) It's not a very nice word
72) They probably did, after the fire
73) Speed it up a little bit
74) They're supposed to wait until there's no traffic
75) The year the first United States transcontinental railroad was completed
76) Blue or gray?
77) He's got the household pets covered
78) The town was along Blaine the Mono's route
79) Think: David Bowie
80) Not the kind for pets, though
81) They give 'em away at restaurants. Mmmm . . . leftovers!
82) Perhaps because a character already has that name
83) There weren't that many left living
84) Thc "narrator" is an obvious nod
85) Nearly a dozen at last count
86) Uh, oh
87) The answer surprised me, too
88) He writes a regular column for *Cemetery Dance*
89) Graffiti features prominently in the story
90) Co-star of *Christine*
91) He was also in *Babe* and one of the *Star Trek* films
92) Both of them were terrible
93) Call him Sir Tony
94) Another common feature: King didn't cameo in any of them
95) He looked somewhat Amish
96) Pre-production stopped and started several times in 2004
97) Morgan Freeman co-starred
98) The character's first name has some significance, too

99) One of them was a retread of his *Storm of the Century* cameo
100) *The Dead Zone* TV series and *Riding the Bullet* were also filmed here

CHAPTER 8: NON-FICTION BOOKS, ESSAYS, REVIEWS, COLUMNS AND LIVE APPEARANCES

1) Dedication in *Danse Macabre*
2) Could be the subtitle to *Watership Down*
3) House number 665 or 667
4) Apparently just a can wasn't big enough
5) Like a German beer mug
6) Calling Captain Ahab
7) His fellow Rock Bottom Remainderette
8) For a book with f-Stop Fitzgerald
9) Also featured in *The Regulators*
10) They did theme music for *Pet Sematary*
11) All the better to see you with
12) Think deeply and you will find the answer diligently
13) Ah, to be young and in love—instead of just in love
14) The curse of the Bambino
15) Author of a book whose working title was *Dear Stephen King*
16) A risk of lightning
17) Three chords and an attitude
18) Abracadbra
19) They're working on a Broadway musical, though
20) Et tu?
21) Hope he got some sleep along the way
22) It represents a major theme in many of his books
23) The last thing you want to have happen to your book
24) It went on the Mayflower
25) Bet he wishes it were B
26) Please phrase your answer in the form of a question
27) Nevermore!
28) I am not making this up
29) Half a dozen bonus points if you can name them
30) This person has never been in a King movie
31) Can you hear me?
32) Two of the titles make this answer obvious when you think about it
33) Combines literacy and soccer
34) The movie wasn't based on it

35) This person also dances backstage at the shows
36) She must have been desperate
37) Audio book narrator
38) aka Dallas Mayr

CHAPTER 9: MISCELLANEOUS

1) Not all, but most
2) An early collection
3) The only limited edition of a Bachman book
4) Pictures of the awards ceremony were taken with a Polaroid camera
5) King plays one
6) Maybe a bat hung from it
7) A very sick person
8) From *People, Places, Things*
9) Inspired by *The Talisman* and other works
10) It's his version of Roland that King sees when he writes
11) A favorite of Greta Shaw
12) Maybe he was sick with a road virus
13) Not everything he writes gets produced or published
14) The Teddy Bear of Horror?
15) He does a wicked Maine aksent
16) Featured in a recent movie and sequel
17) Match the hotel to the film
18) Contributed by a fan who was there
19) Everything has to be condensed to fit in
20) Survived by wife Claudia Inez
21) Play it again, Sam
22) King "co-authored" a short story with him
23) A low number for a limited edition
24) One of my favorite submitted questions
25) Ever et raw meat?
26) They're based in Massachusetts

ANSWERS

Chapter 1: Biography

1) c. Portland
2) c. Edwin
3) b. Donald and Ruth
4) b. Spansky
5) c. Door-to-door vacuum cleaner salesman
6) a. David
7) b. 1947
8) c. Indiana and Connecticut
9) d. Fort Wayne
10) d. Heart Break Hotel
11) b. Mr. Rabbit Trick
12) a. His mother
13) d. Charlie Starkweather
14) d. 7
15) d. The Ritz
16) a. Dave's Rag
17) d. Chris Chesley
18) c. Lisbon Falls
19) b. The Village Vomit
20) a. "I Was a Teenage Grave Robber"
21) a. 1967

22) c. Tabitha
23) c. Spruce
24) b. 1971
25) d. In college
26) d. Jim Bishop
27) d. Teacher's credentials
28) b. Hampden Academy
29) b. Teach High School
30) a. History
31) d. Naomi, Joe, Owen
32) a. Moth
33) d. William Thompson
34) c. A hair dryer
35) c. $400,000
36) c. John Swithen
37) c. Philtrum Press
38) c. 1981
39) d. *Rebecca*
40) b. US
41) d. 31-40
42) d. Shawn T. Mansfield Stadium
43) d. 1997
44) a. Scribner
45) c. Richard Bachman
46) c. Stephanie Spruce
47) d. Bangor West All Stars
48) c. 1999
49) d. A light
50) b. Page 49
51) d. *The Ideal, Genuine Man*
52) d. "Riding the Bullet"
53) a. He wanted to devote more time to scaring his children
54) c. A ghostly room at the Inn
55) b. 25-35
56) d. It is the tale, not he who tells it

CHAPTER 2: NOVELS

1) d. White
2) a. Delores Vickery
3) b. *Cujo*

4) d. *Blaze*
5) b. Detroit
6) a. Birdie
7) c. A pigeon
8) a. Anthony Perkins
9) c. Boston Red Sox
10) b. Jim Morrison
11) c. *True Tales of Demon Infestations*
12) d. Exercise
13) d. Kenny Ray Linkous
14) b. *The Dark Half*
15) b. Limousine driver
16) d. Spring Ball
17) a. Naomi Rachel King
18) c. Penobscot
19) c. Silver
20) b. Johanna Noonan
21) b. George Hatfield
22) d. *It*
23) a. Mother Abagail
24) c. Ben Hanscom
25) b. Harris Avenue Old Crocks
26) c. Josie and the Moonglows
27) b. Mark V. Ziesing Books
28) b. Niner
29) b. 85%
30) c. Mahout
31) a. Nate Hoppenstand
32) b. William
33) d. E
34) d. National Book Award
35) a. Bat
36) c. Rudy Sparkman
37) b. $540
38) d. Bradley Roach
39) d. Cat
40) a. Lester
41) a. Maui
42) c. The Village Café
43) b. *The Dead Zone*
44) a. The Agincourt
45) c. Glen

46) b. Head Selectman
47) a. Junction City
48) c. Giving birth
49) a. Arnette, Texas
50) a. September 21st
51) d. 'Salem's Lot
52) d. John Daniel Torrance
53) d. Ray Van Allen
54) c. Jorgen chainfall
55) a. Wendy Yarrow
56) d. 104
57) d. He cut off his left ear
58) a. 3:05
59) d. Spot
60) b. *The Napkins*
61) c. A human hand
62) b. Visions
63) b. Sonny Singer
64) d. *Black House*
65) c. Harley
66) d. Costello Avenue
67) c. The army
68) b. *The Girl Who Loved Tom Gordon*
69) c. Six
70) d. *It*
71) c. Peter
72) a. Los Zapatos, Mexico
73) a. *The Stand*
74) d. April 14, 1965
75) c. Hit by a motorcycle
76) d. Tiger stripe
77) b. Radamanthus
78) a. Debbie Gehringer
79) a. Bacon
80) c. McDonald's hamburger
81) d. *Cancer*
82) a. Brandon Milheron
83) c. Donald Merwin Elbert
84) c. Rogan
85) d. To be a director
86) b. Saint Christopher's medal
87) c. Winning Ticket

88) c. Irv Manders
89) c. Joe Wyzer
90) a. Pratt, Kansas
91) d. *Fast Cars*
92) b. Code D
93) a. Robert
94) c. Western Maine Realty and Insurance
95) b. His left arm
96) b. *Whispers*
97) b. Douglas Cavell
98) d. Pixel Easel
99) b. October 4, 1993
100) d. 3 inches
101) a. *Rolling Stone* magazine
102) a. Ben Hanscom
103) c. A business card
104) d. Boulder
105) a. Tak
106) b. Trisha McFarland
107) a. Morgan of Orris
108) d. He was shot by one of the officers of Troop D
109) a. Leigh Cabot
110) d. Home rolled cigarettes
111) a. Charlie Merrill
112) b. All his G. I. Joes
113) c. Charlie McGee
114) a. V.C. Andrews
115) b. The Alhambra
116) a. Charity
117) a. *Zenith Rising*
118) d. *The Dead Zone*
119) c. Mr. Jingles
120) b. Selena
121) d. Orrington
122) d. Novril
123) b. Spruce
124) c. Dorcas
125) a. A crow
126) b. Royal
127) d. $500 bill
128) d. Terry
129) b. Menlo Park, New Jersey

130) d. *'Salem's Lot*
131) c. Tony
132) a. He was a dentist
133) d. 4.5 years
134) a. Polly Chalmers
135) d. PARROTHEAD
136) b. An earthquake
137) b. Alexis Machine
138) b. Stephen King's father, Donald
139) a. Actress
140) c. Charlie Pickering
141) a. Adrian Mellon
142) c. Twice
143) a. The language of the unformed
144) c. Henry Montez
145) d. If You Puke, You Pay
146) b. Baby Factory
147) a. Detterick
148) c. Kirsten
149) b. *'Salem's Lot*
150) a. Not a very nice guy
151) a. A baseball card
152) c. Red Razberry Zingers
153) d. Her babysitter assaulted her
154) a. Faye Chapin
155) c. *The Golden Dog*
156) a. Grateful Dead
157) a. *The Stand*
158) a. Carlos Detweiller
159) b. Dorrance Marstellar
160) c. Bangor, Maine
161) a. Theft of services
162) c. Project Blue
163) b. *The Girl Who Loved Tom Gordon*
164) b. Under a stone in the hearth
165) d. *Wizards* and *The Lord Of The Rings* cartoons
166) a. "Misery's Hobby"
167) b. Dorcas
168) b. 36
169) d. *Cujo*
170) c. *Storm of the Century*
171) c. Stan

172) a. Masturbate on it
173) c. Kingsland Ale
174) d. *Hearts in Atlantis*
175) c. Arthritis
176) b. Peter
177) b. *Firestarter*
178) c. $63
179) b. Dark Score Lake
180) c. Sarah Bracknell
181) b. Delain
182) b. She cuts off his foot with an axe
183) b. Army Tech Sergeant
184) d. Both Harold and the Torrances at some point lived on Arapahoe Street in Boulder
185) c. 1958 Plymouth Fury
186) c. *Needful Things*
187) b. Big Steve
188) b. Ford Pinto
189) a. Little Tall Island
190) d. A two-headed parrot
191) d. Cadillac El Dorado
192) a. December 28, 1985
193) b. "Sympathy for the Devil"
194) b. Richie Tozier
195) c. Crysilda Berryman
196) b. 19
197) b. Raymond Andrew Joubert
198) c. She had reduced liver function
199) d. Milky Way
200) c. 3
201) b. The Red King
202) d. Nevada
203) a. Dragon Sand
204) a. Jason Varitek
205) b. Six
206) b. "Our God is strong, our God is with us"
207) d. Three card monte
208) c. *Out Of The Silent Planet*
209) b. Indigo Girls
210) c. Tommy Woodbine
211) a. Irwin Goldman
212) d. Sofa

213) a. *Butch Cassidy and the Sundance Kid*
214) c. A crack appeared in the windshield
215) b. Leland Gaunt's car
216) c. 96
217) d. All of the above
218) a. Jade of the Orient
219) b. Los Angeles
220) a. Conifer Place
221) b. Steamboat Willy
222) c. *The Talisman*
223) a. Greg Stillson
224) b. April Fool's Day
225) b. *Delight* and *Song of the Hammer*
226) c. Maine
227) d. Temporarily elevated
228) d. She squashed it with a plunger
229) b. *It*
230) a. *Needful Things*
231) d. *Conway's Daughter*
232) a. *Being Two*
233) c. Stroke
234) c. Christian Heinrich
235) c. *The Eyes Of The Dragon*
236) d. Dr. Litchfield
237) b. Midnight blue
238) c. Dog
239) a. *Dolores Claiborne*
240) a. George Brannock
241) b. Lot Six
242) d. Melinda Moores
243) d. Teacher
244) c. Harry Auster
245) b. Fort Lauderdale
246) a. U-Haul
247) a. Blue Ribbon Laundry
248) a. Bill McGovern
249) d. Jess Rider
250) c. The Outer Limits
251) d. Two dollars
252) d. Charlie Campion
253) c. West Side Gardeners
254) b. James

255) a. Johns Hopkins
256) a. Stephen King
257) b. Travelin' Jack
258) b. *The Dead Zone*
259) d. Ran into a mailbox post with her bike
260) d. Africa
261) d. Woodleigh
262) c. North to Canada
263) b. Tom Cullen
264) a. Carrie White eats shit
265) a. Lois Chasse
266) d. July 20
267) b. *It*
268) c. Police lieutenant
269) c. Louis Creed
270) c. Cold Mountain Prison
271) a. Children of Jesus Christ Orphanage in Des Moines
272) b. Stu Redman
273) d. Merchant's Bank
274) c. Gives it to an orphanage anonymously
275) a. Mark Petrie
276) d. Mister Dillon
277) d. *Profiles in Courage*
278) c. Don Hagarty
279) d. "Night Journey"
280) a. *Firestarter*
281) a. Robert Ludlum
282) b. Smokey Updike
283) b. Nov 16, 1999-May 29, 2000
284) c. Ferdinand
285) d. Doctor
286) c. Ruth Neary's
287) c. Datsun
288) b. *I was a Teenage Frankenstein*
289) b. It's a long walk back to Eden, sweetheart, so don't sweat the small stuff
290) a. Patricia
291) b. Patrick Danville
292) c. *Needful Things*
293) c. Harold

CHAPTER 3: NOVELLAS

1) b. Ace is Pop's nephew
2) c. "Apt Pupil"
3) d. Berni Wrightson
4) a. American Pride
5) b. Andy Dufresne's prisoner number
6) b. Gordie Lachance
7) b. Kevin Delevan
8) c. "Apt Pupil"
9) d. Fourth of July
10) a. Harlow
11) a. A cuckoo clock
12) a. "Crowfoot Mile"
13) c. Eleusippus Deere and Meleusippus Verrill
14) c. Stevens
15) a. He is the Tarker's Mills werewolf
16) b. Arnie Westrum
17) b. Ray Brower
18) b. Oatley, New York
19) d. "The Sun Dog"
20) d. Flying a kite
21) d. "The Sun Dog"
22) b. The only Newspaper Fairy in Junction City
23) b. John Kintner
24) a. "The Mist"
25) c. Frank
26) b. Solar power
27) c. *When Harry Met Sally*
28) a. Lard Ass
29) a. Linda
30) c. *Lord of The Flies*
31) b. The homeless shelter in "The Library Policeman"
32) b. Vern Tessio
33) a. The werewolf killed only animals instead of people
34) b. "The Breathing Method"
35) d. Twenty $50 bills
36) b. He had a lisp
37) d. Kodak
38) c. *The Inheritors*
39) d. Emlyn McCarron

40) c. New Year's Eve
41) b. Cam
42) d. "The Body"
43) a. Zihuatanejo
44) c. Dorothy McGuire
45) b. Bourbon
46) d. "Secret Window, Secret Garden"
47) b. Linda Ronstadt
48) a. Wisconsin
49) b. April
50) b. Farrah Fawcett
51) d. Months of the year
52) b. Books
53) c. SILENCE!
54) c. Tarker's Mills
55) b. Morton Rainey
56) c. High cholesterol
57) d. "Answering the Call"
58) a. Richard Sifkitz's agent ("Stationary Bike")

CHAPTER 4: SHORT STORIES

1) c. Every 7 years ("Rainy Season")
2) b. L. L. Bean ("Strawberry Spring")
3) d. "Luckey Quarter"
4) c. Camaro ("The Raft")
5) d. Pittsburgh ("The Raft")
6) a. "The Crate" ("Creepshow")
7) b. Carson City, NV ("Luckey Quarter")
8) a. University of Maine Forestry Dept. ("Uncle Otto's Truck")
9) c. Derry ("The Road Virus Heads North")
10) d. Cessna Skymaster 337 N101BL ("The Night Flier")
11) b. Changing his name ("Survivor Type")
12) a. 0
13) c. Castle Rock Newsletter
14) d. "Sorry, Right Number"
15) c. October ("The Raft")
16) d. By a walking windmill ("The Sun Dog")
17) a. They poured lye on his face and fingers ("The Death of Jack Hamilton")
18) c. John Tell

19) c. *Last Dangerous Visions*
20) d. Harlan Ellison
21) d. *Rolling Stone*
22) b. *Skeleton Crew*, Scream Press
23) d. "My Pretty Pony"
24) b. Nose ("Chattery Teeth")
25) c. Oregon ("You Know They Got a Hell of a Band")
26) a. "The Old Dude's Ticker"
27) d. Edgar Allan Poe
28) a. Gourmet foods ("All That You Love Will Be Carried Away")
29) c. Golden Girl ("The Mist")
30) c. "Stationary Bike"
31) b. *Cavalier*
32) b. Peruvian Boomslang ("Autopsy Room Four")
33) b. "Strawberry Spring"
34) a. Alfred Hitchcock
35) d. "Night Surf"
36) b. Chris Chesley
37) c. "1408"
38) b. Boston
39) b. "The Things They Left Behind"
40) d. 1936 ("The Mist")
41) d. Jack Russell Terrier ("L.T.'s Theory of Pets")
42) b. *The New Yorker* and *Esquire*
43) a. Tuesdays and Thursdays ("The Boogeyman")
44) c. "What Tricks Your Eye"
45) a. Whitehead City, Mars ("The Jaunt")
46) d. DEF LEPPARD 4-EVER ("Chattery Teeth")
47) b. Rachel ("The Raft")
48) a. 6 times ("The Ledge")
49) d. Rode ("Riding the Bullet")
50) d. Lucille Ball ("L.T.'s Theory of Pets")
51) c. $35
52) a. Mrs Carmody ("The Mist")
53) b. Electricity ("Quitter's Inc.")
54) a. Darvon ("The Woman in the Room")
55) c. Ophelia ("Mrs. Todd's Shortcut")
56) d. Jonathan Swithen
57) b. Le Palais ("Dedication")
58) d. *Penthouse*
59) d. A painting ("The Road Virus Heads North")
60) c. *Night Shift*

61) b. Lawyer ("The Mist")
62) c. "Riding The Bullet"
63) d. 5000 crowns ("Jhonathan and the Witchs")
64) b. Fourteen
65) a. "Everything's Eventual"
66) a. "The Float" ("The Raft")
67) b. Oh God please help us
68) b. Start naming states ("The Ten O'Clock People")
69) c. Bellis ("The Ballad of the Flexible Bullet")
70) a. Maddie Pace ("Home Delivery")
71) d. Nebraska ("Children of the Corn")
72) a. Cleaves Mills, New Hampshire ("Weeds")
73) c. *Borderlands 5* ("Stationary Bike")
74) b. Oglethorpe Crater
75) c. Conant's Truck Stop ("Trucks")
76) b. A fuck in a rabbit hutch ("Everything's Eventual")
77) c. "The 43rd Dream" and "Code Name: Mousetrap"
78) c. "I've Got to Get Away!"
79) d. Castle Rock
80) c. Richard Dees ("The Night Flier")
81) c. Issue #14 ("Chattery Teeth")
82) b. *Skeleton Crew*
83) b. "1408", "In the Deathroom", "Lunch at the Gotham Café"
84) c. Kurt Cobain ("You Know They Got a Hell of a Band")
85) b. "Stationary Bike"
86) d. "Do the Dead Sing?"
87) d. "All That You Love Will Be Carried Away"
88) b. A drop of blood
89) a. He will be beheaded ("Jhonathan and the Witchs")
90) a. Thunderbird
91) d. "L.T.'s Theory of Pets"
92) b. *The Tommyknockers*
93) c. Mary Theresa Charlton
94) b. "Dolan's Cadillac"
95) c. The Axe Man ("L.T.'s Theory of Pets")
96) d. Black
97) d. "The King Family and the Wicked Witch" (aka: "Farting Cookie")
98) a. Maple duff ("L.T.'s Theory of Pets")
99) b. Arrowhead ("The Mist")
100) b. Fornit Some Fornus ("The Ballad of the Flexible Bullet")
101) b. Goat Island
102) d. Ollie Weeks

103) b. North
104) b. "Harvey's Dream"
105) b. *Night Shift*
106) b. O. Henry
107) d. Both are told in epistolary form
108) c. *Kingdom Hospital*
109) a. "Angie"
110) b. In the Blue Ribbon Laundry ("The Mangler")
111) d. Bangor
112) a. $10,000 ("Battleground")
113) b. Harold Davis High School ("Sometimes They Come Back")
114) b. He ran over a cat with it ("The Lawnmower Man")
115) a. Strawberry double-dip cone ("I Know What You Need")
116) c. "The Last Rung on the Ladder"
117) a. Mr. Norman ("Here There Be Tygers")
118) b. In a box in the attic ("The Monkey")
119) d. "Cain Rose Up"
120) a. Mercedes
121) c. Haven
122) b. Operation Straw ("The Jaunt")
123) d. Victor Carune
124) b. 1927 ("The Wedding Gig")
125) c. Cornet
126) d. Hybrid ("The Word Processor")
127) c. "The Man Who Would Not Shake Hands"
128) a. "The Man Who Would Not Shake Hands"
129) c. "Beachworld"
130) b. Five ("The Reaper's Image")
131) a. Cheryl Craig
132) c. Stranded on a desert island ("Survivor Type")
133) a. The agent
134) b. *Underworld Figures* ("The Ballad of the Flexible Bullet")
135) d. Goose Wallow, Wyoming
136) a. "It Grows On You"
137) a. "A Cask of Amontillado"
138) d. Dolan killed her because she was going to testify against him
139) c. A Nautilus machine ("Dolan's Cadillac")
140) a. Freelance writer ("The End of the Whole Mess")
141) d. Robert Fornoy
142) b. From her brother ("Suffer the Little Children")
143) c. Pittsburgh Penguins
144) d. Gates Falls ("It Grows On You")

145) a. *Rose Red*
146) c. *Blaze of Glory* ("Dedication")
147) a. CPA ("The Moving Finger"
148) d. Jeopardy ("The Moving Finger")
149) c. The Dead Beats ("Sneakers")
150) b. George ("My Pretty Pony")
151) c. 14-60
152) c. Wheel of Fortune ("Sorry, Right Number")
153) d. Bill
154) a. Author ("Sorry, Right Number")
155) c. Peter Straub
156) d. London
157) b. The Bradburys
158) b. Part of a treasure map
159) d. Raymond Chandler
160) a. E-book
161) b. The world's oldest elevator operator ("Umney's Last Case")
162) b. Samuel D. Landry
163) c. Umney's creator
164) b. "Suffer the Little Children"
165) c. Florida
166) b. At a school dance ("That Feeling, You Can Only Say What It Is In French")
167) a. The Dolphin
168) c. 1910
169) d. *Ten Nights in Ten Haunted Churches*
170) c. The Village Voice
171) d. 1414
172) a. Sewing machine salesman

CHAPTER 5: THE BACHMAN BOOKS

1) a. Claudia Inez Eschelman
2) d. 1985
3) d. Cancer of the pseudonym
4) b. Steve Brown
5) a. *The Dark Half*
6) d. *Desperation*
7) c. "Apt Pupil"
8) c. *Misery*
9) b. Guy Pillsbury

10) b. Insomnia
11) a. *Getting it On*
12) d. *The Regulators*
13) d. *Gypsy Pie*
14) b. Placerville High School
15) c. 06-30-00
16) b. Ted Jones
17) c. Bart Dawes
18) d. Olivia
19) c. Manager of the Blue Ribbon Laundry
20) c. Jimmy Laughlin
21) a. Ben Richards
22) c. Jesus
23) b. Cary Ripton
24) a. Poplar
25) c. *The Shining*
26) c. Peter Jackson
27) c. Dream Catcher
28) c. *The Regulators*
29) b. 4 Bullets
30) b. How you kick a football
31) d. 30-30
32) a. May 1st
33) c. 100
34) d. Susanna Lemke
35) d. 47
36) d. Davis
37) b. Peter McVries
38) a. Curley
39) c. Conserve energy whenever possible
40) a. Stebbins
41) d. Sneakers
42) c. 7
43) b. Stebbins
44) d. Danvers
45) d. 1 hour
46) a. Garraty
47) b. The first name of Donald Westlake's pseudonym
48) a. By Billy's weight
49) c. 42 inches
50) b. Lemke
51) d. *Thinner*

52) c. 1972
53) a. 1977
54) b. *The Running Man*
55) b. Sam Peckinpah

CHAPTER 6: THE DARK TOWER SERIES

1) b. *The Magazine of Fantasy and Science Fiction*
2) c. 3000-4000
3) b. 15
4) a. 22
5) a. Johnny Winter
6) c. March
7) b. 1970
8) b. 12
9) c. Robert Browning
10) d. Clifford D. Simak
11) b. Cort
12) b. Cook
13) a. Hax
14) b. Marten
15) a. Berry pies
16) b. Poisoned meat
17) b. To the roof to masturbate
18) a. Gabrielle
19) a. Hanged
20) b. A splinter of wood from the gallows' railing
21) a. Rooks and ravens
22) c. Under Hax's shoes
23) b. 16
24) a. Cort
25) a. 2
26) a. Once
27) b. Twice
28) b. David the hawk
29) b. 14
30) b. West
31) d. Wolf
32) d. *Oedipus Rex*
33) c. Rook's skull
34) c. Dis

35) d. Rusher
36) d. Francis Lengyll
37) c. Dubativo
38) b. Stanley Ruiz
39) c. Christopher Johns
40) a. Fardo
41) c. She feasts on a meal of blood
42) d. Mrs. Beech's
43) d. A reap-charm in the shape of a bell
44) c. Farson's nephew
45) d. The Tower
46) b. South
47) a. Civil War
48) c. Eluria
49) a. Coquina
50) c. Mohaine
51) b. Zoltan
52) d. Raven
53) c. The Lord's Prayer
54) c. Pappa Doc
55) d. Pricetown
56) a. Tull
57) c. Nineteen
58) b. A cloven hoof
59) d. She begs Roland to kill her
60) b. Sheb
61) b. A whore in Tull
62) c. "Hey Jude"
63) b. Mejis
64) b. Star
65) a. Nort
66) a. Sylvia Pittson
67) b. Chambers
68) d. Drugs
69) d. Mescaline
70) a. A jawbone
71) a. Susan
72) d. The jawbone
73) d. Slow
74) a. Rabbit
75) d. Jake
76) a. Baboon

77) c. The Hanged Man
78) c. The Dark Tower
79) d. 10
80) b. *The Drawing of the Three*
81) b. The Western Sea
82) b. Lester
83) a. The Prisoner
84) b. 1987
85) a. Heroin
86) c. Cocaine
87) c. Enrico Balazar
88) c. Henry
89) b. New York
90) a. 3A
91) b. Susy Douglas
92) c. To take a woman by force
93) c. Bartender
94) a. Johnny Cash
95) c. Jack Andolini
96) d. Enrico Balazar
97) c. Nine
98) b. Dennis and Thomas from *The Eyes of the Dragon*
99) b. Dog
100) a. A sandwich
101) c. The Lady of Shadows
102) c. At Macy's
103) b. 1964
104) b. 26
105) a. *The Shining*
106) b. 1959
107) c. A pile of stones
108) c. 3 years
109) b. Dentist
110) b. A brick
111) d. Blue Woman
112) a. Jake
113) a. C.P.A.
114) b. *Shooter's Bible*
115) c. Fat Johnny Holden
116) b. Katz's Drug Store
117) c. Keflex
118) d. A lighter

119) a. Run over by a train
120) a. "The Bear"
121) c. Richard Adams
122) b. Mir
123) b. Radar dish
124) b. Bear-Turtle
125) d. TS Eliot and Robert Browning
126) b. Photo of the Leaning Tower of Pisa colored black
127) d. Playing chess
128) b. 1977
129) d. Elmer
130) a. Bologna and cheese
131) b. Engineer Bob
132) a. Beryl Evans
133) a. Stonehenge
134) c. "Roland! Roland, help me!"
135) b. Oy
136) b. From the way he repeated the word "boy"
137) c. A plane
138) d. In a WWII fighter plane
139) a. A swastika
140) b. Lydia
141) a. Bill and Till
142) b. Deidre the Mad
143) d. Apon
144) a. They were black
145) b. Mercy
146) d. River Crossing
147) c. Huntress Moon
148) c. A revolver and an olive branch
149) a. Pink
150) d. Riddles
151) a. Topeka
152) a. Ardis
153) a. Four
154) c. Alain
155) c. 500
156) b. Black
157) c. "And have a great day!"
158) a. Rocket J. Squirrel
159) c. *Insomnia*
160) b. Candleton

161) b. Takuro Spirit
162) c. Frank Muller
163) b. 12
164) a. Father Callahan
165) b. Faddah
166) a. *'Salem's Lot*
167) a. Topeka, 1982
168) a. Los Zapatos, Mexico
169) c. Ben Mears' funeral
170) a. William Faulkner, Stephen King and Raymond Chandler
171) a. Roland of Gilead
172) b. Shoots out his eyes
173) c. Harry Potter
174) d. Crimson King
175) b. Tabitha King
176) a. 13
177) c. Maturin
178) a. Greta Shaw
179) d. House of Ghosts
180) c. Dennis's Waffles and Pancakes
181) c. Damascus
182) b. Borders
183) a. *Girl, Interrupted* didn't premiere until December 1999
184) d. Park-Plaza Hotel
185) b. Lyndon Johnson
186) c. Body temp
187) c. Swedish Ambassador
188) b. *King Arthur*
189) a. Columbia
190) b. Sixty-first and Lexington
191) c. The Ambush
192) a. Jack Andolini
193) d. Vanderbilt
194) b. Henry Dean's old girlfriend
195) d. Roger Clemens
196) a. 20-25 miles
197) b. Rocket Road
198) c. Bridgton
199) b. Maine State Prison
200) c. $15
201) d. Richard Bachman
202) a. Oxford

203) b. Arc 16 Experimental Station
204) c. Amos
205) c. A NY city cop
206) a. Liquor store
207) d. Kansas Road
208) c. Moses Carver
209) b. Jeep Cherokee
210) a. A folk-singer and guitarist
211) c. Oren
212) b. Dustin Hoffman in *Midnight Cowboy*
213) b. A key
214) a. $39
215) c. Thirty-six months
216) c. A bus was blocking traffic
217) c. $50
218) a. Davis
219) a. July 12, 1977
220) b. Three thousand
221) d. Pops Merrill
222) a. Three years
223) b. Bog Road
224) d. Seventeen
225) a. John Cullum
226) b. Ford Galaxie
227) c. Visit the Statue of Liberty
228) d. Galee
229) a. Chumley
230) c. *The Dead Zone*
231) b. Danny Torrance
232) d. Fifty
233) b. Prison guard
234) c. John Fowles
235) b. Five
236) a. South
237) b. South
238) d. Wendell
239) a. David
240) b. July
241) b. Calvin Tower
242) c. 1992
243) d. *Insomnia*
244) a. Rebecca

245) c. $19,000
246) a. Feemalo
247) b. Two years ago
248) d. XIX

CHAPTER 7: MOVIES, MINISERIES, AND OTHER ADAPTATIONS

1) a. *Dolores Claiborne*
2) c. Andre Linoge
3) c. *Rose Madder*
4) d. Drew Barrymore
5) b. The Dark Man
6) a. *Maximum Overdrive*
7) b. *The Shining*
8) b. "Chattery Teeth"
9) c. Fun Fun Fun (Beach Boys)
10) b. *Cat's Eye*
11) b. Someone using an ATM
12) c. *The Golden Years*
13) a. Leigh Cabot
14) c. Tyson Blue
15) a. *The Golden Years*
16) c. *The Dark Half*
17) d. April
18) c. David Dukes
19) c. *Earth vs. The Flying Saucers*
20) a. "Weird Al" Yankovic
21) c. A marble ashtray with a figure attached
22) c. $70,000
23) a. Curtis
24) a. *The Green Mile* and *Christine*
25) c. AC/DC
26) b. Pizza delivery guy
27) d. 16-20
28) c. Ed Harris
29) c. *The Lawnmower Man*
30) b. The Weather Channel
31) b. *The Legend of Sleepy Hollow*
32) a. Molly Ringwald

33) b. Timothy Daly
34) c. Timothy Hutton
35) b. *Storm of the Century*
36) c. *Pet Sematary*
37) c. A bust of Elvis
38) a. Steamroller
39) d. Horlicks
40) b. *The Stand*
41) b. *Cujo*
42) c. Frank Darabont
43) a. "Weeds"
44) a. Kathy Bates
45) d. Banghor
46) a. Pharmacist
47) c. Frank Darabont
48) a. *Quicksilver Highway*
49) a. 4
50) a. Jordy Verrill
51) b. Winchester Mansion
52) a. We're all dead and this is hell
53) b. *Misery* and *The Golden Years*
54) b. Teddy Weizak
55) b. Kathy Bates
56) a. Outlander, we have your woman!
57) d. An azka
58) c. 1991
59) d. James Wyeth
60) d. *The Stand* and '*Salem's Lot*
61) a. *Maximum Overdrive*
62) b. Minister
63) b. Nozz-A-La Cola
64) a. Captain Trips
65) c. George Thorogood
66) c. Grantham
67) b. Monsters
68) a. "The Woman in the Room"
69) a. *Pet Sematary*
70) d. Antubis
71) c. Chinga
72) d. Gates Falls
73) d. Bus driver
74) a. Drawbridge

75) b. 1869
76) b. Uniforms
77) c. *Cat's Eye* and *Cujo*
78) c. Earl Candleton
79) d. *The Golden Years*
80) b. Cemetery caretaker
81) c. Toothpick
82) b. *Carrie*
83) c. *The Stand*
84) a. Tales from the Crypt
85) d. Stephen King
86) c. *Quantum Leap*
87) a. Jack Kamen
88) a. Bev Vincent
89) d. "All That You Love Will Be Carried Away"
90) a. Keith Gordon
91) c. James Cromwell
92) d. "Trucks"
93) c. *Hearts in Atlantis*
94) a. All were Castle Rock productions
95) b. *Secret Window*
96) b. *The Talisman*
97) a. *The Shawshank Redemption*
98) b. *Carrie von Trier*
99) d. 3
100) c. Vancouver

CHAPTER 8: NON-FICTION BOOKS, ESSAYS, REVIEWS, COLUMNS AND LIVE APPEARANCES

1) b. Here there be Tygers
2) a. "The Jumper"
3) d. "The Neighborhood of the Beast"
4) b. The Garbage Truck
5) b. Joel Stein
6) a. "Fenway and the Great White Whale"
7) c. Amy Tan
8) c. Gargoyles
9) d. Lunchtime Gloop
10) a. The Ramones

11) d. A tiffany vase
12) c. Adverbs
13) d. Seventeen
14) b. Boston Red Sox
15) c. Stewart O'Nan
16) c. It was held at a church
17) b. Guitar
18) c. "Black Magic and Music: A Novelist's Perspective on Bangor"
19) b. John Cougar Mellancamp
20) d. Ides of Mohonk
21) d. *Insomnia*
22) d. Spider web
23) b. It was loaded into a moving truck and hauled back to Maine
24) c. The Rock Bottom Remainders
25) d. JK Rowling
26) c. Backstage before a game show
27) a. A flaming taper and a sinister raven
28) b. Dave Barry
29) d. Six
30) d. Lynn Redgrave
31) b. Teen Angel
32) a. Bo Diddley/ Stand By Me/ You Can't Judge a Book by the Cover
33) c. New England Scores
34) c. *Secret Windows*
35) b. Tabitha King
36) c. She said he stole her ideas for *Desperation*
37) d. Ron McLarty
38) c. *The Crossings* by Jack Ketchum

CHAPTER 9: MISCELLANEOUS

1) d. 23-33
2) b. *Night Shift*
3) c. *The Regulators*
4) a. *Four Past Midnight*
5) a. Guitar
6) c. *Cujo*
7) c. Melinda Moores / *The Green Mile*
8) c. "But Only Darkness Loves Me"
9) d. The Territories
10) b. Michael Whelan

11) b. Inside View
12) b. *999*
13) b. King's screenplay of *Cujo*
14) c. The black #13 with "King of Horror" written on its chest
15) a. *Dreamcatcher*
16) a. The X-Men
17) d. Redrum ELA
18) d. Billerica (Mass. Public Library)
19) b. Adapting his own novels to the screen
20) d. Richard Bachman
21) b. *Casablanca*
22) c. Edgar Allan Poe
23) b. 250
24) d. We don't know, but a lot!
25) c. Dinner with Stephen King
26) d. Lowell Spinners

ILLUSTRATED QUESTIONS

A) Ferdinand, *Rose Madder*
B) *Desperation*
C) *Insomnia*
D) *Dreamcatcher*
E) Jack Torrance
F) *Black House*
G) Gorg, which means "death"
H) Pennywise
I) 1958 Plymouth Fury
J) Buick
K) *The Dark Half*
L) Sara Laughs
M) Joe Claiborne
N) Leland Gaunt
O) 217
P) Wisconsin Highway 35
Q) Annie Wilkes
R) A werewolf
S) George Staub
T) *The Sun Dog*
U) *The Langoliers*
V) "The Rainy Season"

W) “I am the Doorway”
X) “ The Road Virus Heads North”
Y) “Trucks”
Z) “Graveyard Shift”
AA) “Jerusalem’s Lot”
BB) Mrs. Todd
CC) A gypsy’s curse
DD) *The Regulators*
EE) Arthur Eld’s sword, Excalibur
FF) The fifth
GG) In conjunction with nothing else: strength
HH) Walter threw it in the fire
II) He used it to completely cover the Hanged Man card representing Roland
JJ) Removed two fingers and a toe, tore a chunk of meat from his lower calf, destroyed his boots and poisoned him
KK) 18
LL) Marlowe, the Kings’ pet Welsh Corgi
MM) Susannah Dean
NN) Encrypted microburst radio transmissions
OO) Madrigal, Son of a Bitch
PP) Mia, Mother
QQ) 1977
RR) Fra Lippo Lippi
SS) An hourglass, like a female black widow
TT) Taheen
UU) An anteater
VV) Morgan Freeman as Col. Abraham Curtis
WW) Frank Darabont
XX) *Pet Sematary*
YY) *The Dead Zone*
ZZ) eBay
AAA) *Blood and Smoke*
BBB) *It*

AFTERWORD

BY MICHELLE L. REVELLE

SKEMERs Founder/Co-President

SKEMERs is an internet club of more than 2,000 members. We prefer not to be called a "fan club," since we go above and beyond the appreciation of Stephen King.

In the fall of 1995, I had just gotten internet access. I had been an avid King fan and collector for over five years by that time and was looking to join some type of discussion group or club. What I found were message boards, chats and web pages. They were great, but just didn't provide the interaction I wanted. I had always regretted that I became a fan too late to be a part of the Castle Rock newsletter. I wanted to "meet" people from all over the world, find out more about upcoming King events and releases, and talk about the books in detail. Unfortunately, there wasn't much available.

On one AOL message board I found a post from a woman named Missy Gongre. She was looking to start an email newsletter club called "Rose Madder", after her favorite King book. I quickly emailed Missy and told her that I would not only like to join, but that I would like help in any capacity. We launched the group together with a membership of three. She became the President/Newsletter Monitor and I became the Vice President/Recruiter. Her job was to compile and email the newsletter daily. I found various ways of promoting our new newsletter. In the months that followed, the membership grew.

After a few weeks and less than a dozen members, I suggested a name change. Rose Madder didn't really seem like a fitting name. What I had come up with was SKEMERs—**S**tephen **K**ing **E-M**ail**ERs**. Everyone agreed that it was a great name and thus the name stuck! As the group grew, a Free Zone Committee was created to handle various jobs that became necessary: First Edition Expert ("The Gauntster"), AOL Message Board Monitor, Conference Planners ("Roadwork Crew"), etc.

Missy and I always agreed our newsletter would not only be a forum to discuss King. We wanted to be a club with heart—somewhere you'd go to make friends. Quickly, it became that and much, much more. The members of SKEMERs became a family. We've celebrated weddings and births, grieved over deaths and illnesses, consoled those that needed a shoulder to cry on, and lent an ear to whatever news someone had to share. We've even had two marriages that have happened as a result of the friendships created.

Months passed and Missy became too busy for the newsletter. I took on her duties and became known affectionately as "The Dictator" since I was handling a lot of things myself. When the group reached its 1,000-member mark, I realized I needed help so I asked fellow member, Brad Jahn, to be my second-in-command. He assisted me during computer outages, vacations, and mental burnouts. Remember, it's a daily newsletter. Every day there was work to be done on some aspect of SKEMERs.

When our original website by Michael McAlcin just didn't seem to be working for us, one of our members offered to make some changes. Michele Ballard and her husband Andrew redesigned and revamped our website, moving it to its current home at www.skemers.com. They have donated so much of their own time and money into this project and the outcome is a web page that also services as our member database and email program. This facilitates the sending of the newsletter. No longer did I have to review cancellations and name changes before creating the letter.

Everything was now handled automatically. The members also had an area of their own to list their interests and geographical information.

Another great thing about SKEMERs is our yearly conference. In the past we've had small gatherings throughout the country to meet fellow members. In chat one night, someone suggested having a conference so that a larger group could meet. The yearly SKEMERs conference was born. Each year, a percentage of us get together in King's hometown of Bangor, Maine. The first one in 1997 was so magical. To see a group of 75 people come together in one place to enjoy each other's company was a wonderful moment for me. It showed me just how much SKEMERs meant to everyone. Stephen King's books came alive for us as we visited locations that had inspired the geography of his books. We were also fortunate enough to be the first people to purchase *Dark Tower IV: Wizard & Glass.* In 2003, members trekked to Estes Park, Colorado to spend the weekend in the hotel that inspired King to write *The Shining.* Every Halloween weekend, the Stanley Hotel hosts a costume ball. Several of our members were fortune enough to place in the contest!

In 2001, I became pregnant with my daughter, Tessa. I knew that having a child would take me away from much of my SKEMERs responsibilities, so I asked Christopher Champine to Co-President. He would take charge of the Newsletters and assist in the day-to-day functions of the group. He has become all of that and more. Also, with her great ideas and talent, Michele Ballard, has become the third side to our governing triangle. We help make important decisions together, share the responsibilities, and try to keep things going smoothly. There's a lot of behind-the-scenes work for a group our size!

Now that I work full-time and my daughter is a toddler, my free time is almost nil. I don't have as much time for the group as I once had, but it still holds a special place in my heart. The friendship mentality of the group still holds true, these nine years later. I am honored that such a good thing has lasted for as long as it has. I hope the magic that has brought us together can last another nine years. For its members, SKEMERs will always hold a special place in their hearts.

For more information on our group, please visit our web page at www.skemers.com.

ACKNOWLEDGEMENTS

The following people contributed trivia questions to this volume. In many ways, this is their book as much as it is ours, and we'd like to thank them for their contributions:

Nassim Abed, Patty Andersen, Dawn R. Baker, Stephen Bamberg, James Beach, Frank Benefield Jr., Michael Bernstein, David Beutel, Tyson Blue, Meridith Bolster, Ariel Bosi, Kenneth Bradford, Ramonda Brady, Emil Brodsky, Robin Bruner, Kimberly Carter, Mary Theresa Charlton, Keith Clark, Cheryl "CJ" Clickstein, Alan Combe, Kirsty Deans, Steven Delman, Paquito David DelRio, Rich DeMars, Lisa Durant, Sunny Cheong Kai Fei, Chris Fell, Elizabeth M. Fenner, Jacques Filippi, Brent Foehl, Phillip Frangules, Anne Frifelt, Alex Gadd, Victoria Gaudette, Tyler Hall, Shawn E. Hale, James Hardy, David Heath, Debi Hildenbrand, Lisa Ann Hill, Brian Hilton, Jennifer M. Hogan, Tina Hospers, Janet Hull, Bob Ireland, Anita Jessen, Brandy Joyce, Thomas J. Kemock, Sharon King, Tomas Krynsky, Jason Kyriacou, Michael Anthony Lee, Jana Long, Carrie Lubiniecki, Linda Mallon, Ayesha Martin, Barbara McCollum, Wayne McCormack, Sue Meeks, Heather Meyer, Victor and Rosandra Montequin, Victoria Moore, Scott Morris, Kay Moss,

Michael Myers, Jim Nassivera, Terry Newsom, Michael Noble, Tammy Noeske, Renee Oakes, Jimmy Olsson, Lucie A Pecor, Marty Petosa, Thomas Phillips, Eva Quisenberry, Kevin Michael Rohde, Lisa Rowley, Timothy Ryan, Debora Sambol, Steve Savile, Susan Sawicki, Justin R. Schulke, Ric Schuster, Russell Schwartz, Robert Scott, Sheridan Shields, William Smith, Terry W. Smith, Areia Spinner, Sierra Starnes, Justin Tate, Thomas Teigen, Terry Tidwell, Lou Van Hille, Christine Vanaman, Mark Vincze, Ruth Volpe, Billie Weese, Nate Westbury, Michael Wadden, Debra Wimer, William Wold, Rocky Wood, Rachael Wright, Amy Zillner, and David Zipp.

ABOUT THE EDITORS

BEV VINCENT has been a Contributing Editor with *Cemetery Dance* magazine since early 2000, where he writes the regular column "News from the Dead Zone" and conducts the occasional interview. He is also a book critic with the *Conroe* (Texas) *Courier* and the author of over two dozen peer-reviewed scientific articles. His short fiction has appeared in *Cemetery Dance*, *Shivers II*, *Borderlands 5*, *Who Died in Here?* and numerous other magazines and anthologies. His first book-length work, the Stephen King authorized *The Road to the Dark Tower*, was published by New American Library in 2004.

He lives in southeast Texas with his wife and soon-to-be college-bound daughter. He is currently working on a novel, another non-fiction book, several book reviews, a *Cemetery Dance* column, maintaining his web page (www.BevVincent.com), writing a few short stories and contemplating a novella. All in his spare time.

BRIAN FREEMAN founded StephenKingNews.com while in high school, and his Stephen King News mailing list is now the largest on the web that is not run by King or his publishers. The website receives well over a million hits a year.

His short fiction has been published in *From The Borderlands,* all three volumes in the *Shivers* series, and many other publications. His new novella *Blue November Storms* will be published as the 14th entry in the Cemetery Dance Novella Series.

Brian Freeman's first novel was recently published in mass market paperback by Leisure and in hardcover by Cemetery Dance Publications under the pen name James Kidman. More novels are on the way.

He can be reached on the web at BrianFreeman.com.

GLENN CHADBOURNE's illustrations have appeared in over twenty books, as well as numerous magazines and comics. His trademark pen and ink drawings have accompanied the works of todays top genre authors. Glenn lives in Newcastle, Maine with his wife, Sheila, and their pug dog, Rocket.